The Morning S
JOURNAL
Vol. 14

MW00906875

Editor: Rick Joyner
Contributing Editors: Jack Deere, Francis Frangipane, Dudley Hall
Managing Editor: Deborah Joyner Johnson
Project Manager: Dana Zondory
Layout and Design: Micah Davis, Dana Zondory
Copy Editors: Roger Hedgspeth, Mike Roberts, Deborah Williams

The Morning Star Journal® USPS012-903 is published quarterly, 4 issues per year, by MorningStar Publications, Inc. A division of MorningStar Fellowship Church, P.O. Box 440, Wilkesboro, NC 28697. Spring 2004 issue. Periodicals postage rates paid at North Wilkesboro, NC and additional mailing offices. CPC Agreement #1472593. ISSN# 10832122

POSTMASTER: Send address corrections to *The Morning Star Journal*®, P.O. Box 440, Wilkesboro, NC 28697

Subscription rates: One year $16.95; Outside U.S. $24.95 USD.

Cover Photo: Eagle Cap Wilderness, Oregon by Matt Peterson

MorningStar Publications is a non-profit organization dedicated to the promulgation of important teachings and timely prophetic messages to the church. We also attempt to promote interchange between the different streams and denominations in the body of Christ.

To receive a subscription to *The Morning Star Journal*®, send payment along with your name and address to *MorningStar Publications*, P.O. Box 440, Wilkesboro, NC 28697, (336) 651-2400 (1-800-542-0278—Credit Card Orders Only); fax (336) 651-2430. One year (4 quarterly issues) U.S. $16.95; Outside U.S. $24.95 USD. Prices are subject to change without notice.

Reprints—Photocopies of any part of the contents of this publication may be made freely. However, to re-typeset information, permission must be requested in writing from *MorningStar Publications Department*, P.O. Box 440, Wilkesboro, NC 28697

BIOS

Wade Taylor is the founder and former president of Pinecrest Bible Training Center in Salisbury Center, New York. He currently edits the quarterly publication, *The Banner.* He is the author of numerous tracts and articles and has written two books available through MorningStar, *The Secret of the Stairs,* and *Waterspouts of Glory.* He travels extensively, ministering in churches and conferences.

Bob Mumford is a dynamic Bible teacher with a unique and powerful gift for imparting the Word of God. Since 1954, thousands of Christians worldwide have attributed their spiritual growth and determination to follow Jesus Christ to his prophetic teaching, helping them understand Father God and His kingdom. Bob has been a spiritual "Papa" to thousands of Christians and his writings have been translated into many different languages. He seeks to bring about personal spiritual change and growth in the life of every believer. Bob can be reached at Lifechangers, P.O. Box 98088, Raleigh, NC, 27624 or call (800) 521-5676 / www.lifechangers.org.

Rick Joyner is the founder, executive director, and senior pastor of MorningStar Fellowship Church. Rick is a well-known author of more than thirty books, including his latest, *The Torch and the Sword,* the long awaited sequel to *The Final Quest* and *The Call,* and his soon to be published, *The Apostolic Church.* He also oversees MorningStar's School of Ministry, Fellowship of Ministries, and Fellowship of Churches. Rick and his wife, Julie, live in North Carolina with their five children: Anna, Aaryn, Amber, Ben, and Sam.

Mike Roberts is originally from the Charlotte, North Carolina area and has been involved at MorningStar for about ten years. He is a graduate of the MorningStar School of Ministry, and has a heart for the prophetic ministry and teaching. Mike is currently on staff at MorningStar Publications and Ministries and lives in Moravian Falls, North Carolina.

Deborah Joyner Johnson is the managing editor of the Publications Department and oversees all publishing projects for MorningStar Publications and Ministries. She shares with her brother, Rick Joyner, a desire to see the body of Christ provided with the highest quality spiritual food that is relevant for our times. Deborah's first book, *The Chosen Path,* was recently released through MorningStar. She has a gifted teaching ministry and shares at conferences and women's groups. Deborah has three children: Matthew, Meredith, and Abby.

Hombre Liggett is ordained through MorningStar Fellowship of Ministries and is the founding pastor of Church of the Harvest, located in Dover, Ohio. Hombre's heart is to lead the members of the body of Christ into prophetic worship, equipped to fulfill their purpose, and provide a platform for them to function. The foundation of his twelve-year ministry is the love of God and the unity of the Spirit.

Cary Summers is the founder and CEO of the Nehemiah Group, a group of companies which provide consulting for profit and nonprofit organizations in strategic planning, organization, operation issues, and transitional planning. Mr. Summers has lectured and spoken internationally and domestically on such topics as leadership principles based on the book of Nehemiah, the relationship of private business and public government sectors, tourism, entrepreneurship and how to create memories worth repeating in retail. Cary and his wife, Jacque, live in Springfield, Missouri and have two children and two grandchildren.

Robin McMillan is currently pastoring the MorningStar Fellowship Church in Charlotte, North Carolina. With a unique preaching style, prophetic giftings, and a desire for the release of God's power, many are impacted by Robin's ministry. Robin and his wife, Donna, live in North Carolina with their four children: John Mark, Christopher, Andy, and Katy.

John Paul Jackson is the founder and chairman of Streams Ministries International located in North Sutton, New Hampshire. A popular teacher and conference speaker, John Paul travels around the world teaching on prophetic gifts, dreams, visions, and the realm of the supernatural. His newest publication, *Moments With God Dream Journal,* offers a unique approach to dream recording. To order his books and tapes, please call 1-888-441-8080, or visit his website at www.streamsministries.com.

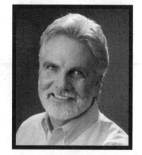

Francis Frangipane is the senior pastor of River of Life Ministries in Cedar Rapids, Iowa, and the president of Advancing Church Ministries. The Lord has used Francis to unite thousands of pastors in prayer in hundreds of cities. With more than a million copies of his best selling books in print, and with an expanding radio and television ministry called "In Christ's Image," Francis is in much demand worldwide. His newest book is entitled, *It's Time to End Church Splits.*

BIOS

Dudley Hall is president of Successful Christian Living Ministries, a ministry dedicated to the restoration of the individual and the church according to God's original plan. As a teacher and popular conference speaker within the body of Christ, Dudley shares the truths which God has imparted to him simply and concisely, offering practical insights to enable believers to grow in their relationships with Christ. Dudley is the author of numerous books, which titles include *Grace Works, A Treasure Worth the Effort,* and *Incense and Thunder.* He and his wife, Betsy, live in Texas with their two children: David and Karis.

Becky Fischer has been in children's ministry for more than ten years. For two of those years she was the children's pastor for MorningStar Fellowship in Wilkesboro. She currently directs, *Kids in Ministry International,* which focuses on training children and children's workers around the world for the work of the ministry. Becky lives in North Dakota.

John Hansen is the accounting manager for MorningStar Fellowship Church. As a former pastor, educator, and financial analyst, it is his heart to help equip people for their church or marketplace callings. John also graduated from the MorningStar School of Ministry, and resides in North Carolina with his wife Lisa and daughter Moriah.

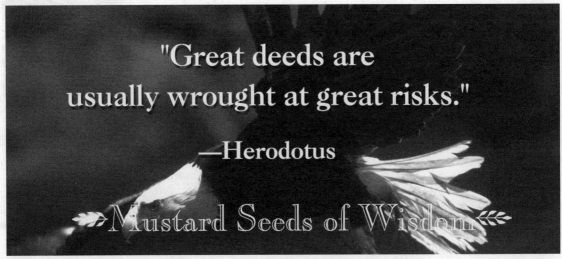

"Great deeds are usually wrought at great risks."

—Herodotus

Mustard Seeds of Wisdom

Maintaining Our Spirituality

All Scriptures are King James Version.

by Wade E. Taylor

> But we speak the wisdom of God in a mystery, even the hidden wisdom, which God ordained before the world unto our glory (I Corinthians 2:7).

The greatest gift and blessing we have is our spiritual hunger. This hunger, along with our spiritual sensitivity, which is the abiding prophetic anointing that enables us to unlock and understand the mysteries within the Word of God, are two of our greatest treasures. Both of these will gradually fade until we are left spiritually barren, unless we maintain a time of active, daily communion and fellowship with our Lord.

> Even the youths shall faint and be weary, and the young men shall utterly fall: But they that wait upon the LORD shall renew their strength…" (Isaiah 40:30-31).

To maintain our spirituality, it is essential that we set apart a specific time and place in which to **"wait upon the Lord,"** and then wait in His presence. As we do this, we will be recharged spiritually, and built-up in our ability to understand and function in spiritual things. Just as a battery has been discharged through use and must be recharged, so also, we must hold ourselves before the Lord in His presence to allow His life and power to flow back into our being.

These times of specific "waiting upon the Lord" will impart to us a divine strength, which replaces our human weakness. This will increase our love for the Lord Himself, and produce within us the anointing that will quicken our understanding, enabling us to respond to spiritual things.

The secret of the LORD is with them that fear Him; and He will show them His covenant (Psalm 25:14).

This word, **"fear"** speaks of a reverential awe, or respect that stimulates us to respond to His presence and "wait upon Him" with focused, undivided attention.

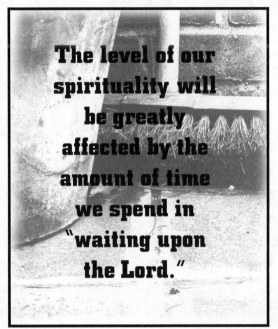

The level of our spirituality will be greatly affected by the amount of time we spend in "waiting upon the Lord."

The Natural and the Spiritual

It is important for us to recognize that we function on two different levels of life. **"It is sown a natural body; it is raised a spiritual body. There is a natural body, and there is a spiritual body" (I Corinthians 15:44.)** Either one or the other of these will predominate— the **"natural,"** or the **"spiritual."** As our spiritual life increases, our carnal desires will decrease. The strength of each of these is determined by the choices we make, the preferences we keep, and what we nurture with our thoughts and actions.

The level of our spirituality will be greatly affected by the amount of time we spend in "waiting upon the Lord." This time spent in waiting is not to be passive, but rather an active waiting in *anticipation*, as one who watches for someone to enter a room. It should include a time of *quiet worship*. This is best expressed by holding the palms of our hands upward toward the Lord in an attitude of receiving spiritual impartation and enabling, along with the expectancy of His coming to commune with us.

As we continue in our "waiting upon the Lord" to receive the impartation of the spiritual life and strength essential to our spiritual well-being, there must be a parallel crucifixion of our natural, soulish life. This is accomplished as we commit to the cross all things which are contrary to our spiritual development and which seek to hinder or replace our times of waiting before the Lord.

As we actively wait in His presence, the Lord will, through this process of crucifixion, remove the agitations, and all that rebels against our becoming still before Him. We must pass through this time of processing before we will be able to fully experience the release of spiritual life which the Lord desires to make available to us.

Our ability to **"wait upon the Lord"** will increase as we **"wait upon the Lord."** As desirable and well-intentioned as they may be, relationships with other Christians will never satisfy our spiritual hunger. There must be the lifting of our being into a vertical relationship with the Lord—an intimate, personal, coming to the Lord Himself, as coming to a person who desires to be known. As we wait in His presence, He will make Himself known to us. Then we will be better able to fellowship one with another.

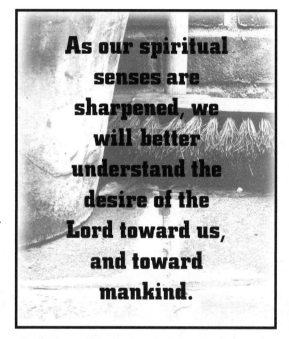

As our spiritual senses are sharpened, we will better understand the desire of the Lord toward us, and toward mankind.

Jesus said: **"But you, when you pray, go into your room, and when you have shut your door, pray to your Father who is in the secret place; and your Father who sees in secret will reward you openly"** (Matthew 6:6 NKJV).

In our Christian experience, it is essential that we set apart special times when we are absolutely alone with the Lord as stated in Revelation 3:20, **"I…will come in to him, and will sup with him, and he with me."**

In "waiting upon the Lord" we are both quickened and lifted into the realm of spiritual life and reality. While we wait, the Lord works, reorienting our desires and creating within us a sensitivity and openness to the "realm of the Spirit."

Not even a two-edged sword can divide between soul and spirit (see Hebrews 4:12). The two are so closely intertwined that only the Lord can separate one from the other. This separation takes place as we spend time in His presence, "waiting upon Him."

As our spiritual senses are sharpened, we will better understand the desire of the Lord toward us, and toward mankind. As a result, we will be eager to enter into a relationship of daily communion with the Lord—in the outworking of His desire for us, and then in cooperative fellowship with Him—the outworking of His purposes for others.

"That I may know him, and the power of his resurrection, and the fellowship of His sufferings, being made conformable unto his death" (Philippians 3:10).

This increased spiritual sensitivity, which we receive through our extended times of "waiting upon the Lord," will also cause us to become more sensitized to the natural realm. We must learn how to bear this sensitivity, without any reaction or retaliation because of what we see or feel.

"Who is blind but my servant? or deaf, as my messenger that I sent? Who is blind as he that is perfect, and blind as the Lord's servant? Seeing many things, but thou observest not; opening the ears, but he heareth not" (Isaiah 42:19-20).

Because of the keen spiritual sensitivity which Jesus possessed, He knew the hearts of men, but He refused to react according to circumstances. He maintained His position in the heavenlies and was motivated according to what His Father was saying and doing, not man.

"Howbeit that was not first which is spiritual, but that which is natural; and afterward that which is spiritual" (I Corinthians 15:46).

As we begin to **"wait upon the Lord,"** we may "feel" very little of Him, or of His presence. But as we continue to "wait before Him" in the light of the expectancy we have, we will pass from the natural realm into the spiritual where we become acutely aware of the Lord, and of His presence.

We are to move in the faith we have, and then, we will be lifted upward into the "realm of the Spirit" where, with prophetic understanding, we will begin to move into that which is spiritual. It is essential that we set apart time within the schedule of our busy lives to **"wait upon the Lord."** We will never be disappointed if we do. ■

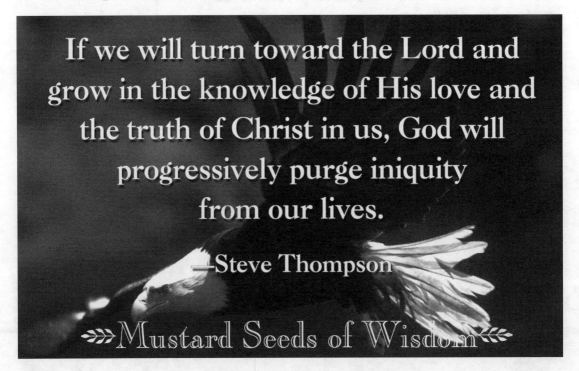

If we will turn toward the Lord and grow in the knowledge of His love and the truth of Christ in us, God will progressively purge iniquity from our lives.

—Steve Thompson

⇒⇒⇒ Mustard Seeds of Wisdom ⇐⇐⇐

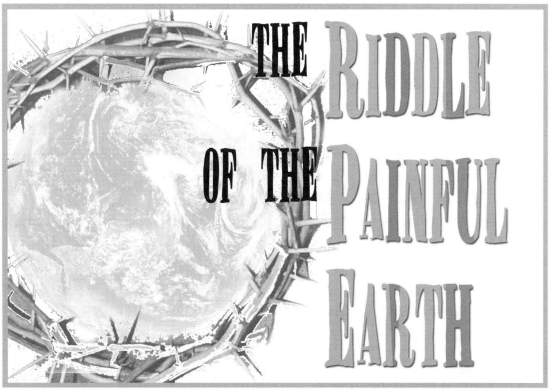

THE RIDDLE OF THE PAINFUL EARTH

by Bob Mumford

Easter is a very special time of the year. We celebrate the triumphal entry of Jesus into Jerusalem, as well as His painful death, and glorious resurrection. Easter is an important time for me personally because it is when the Lord reclaimed me after being backslidden for twelve years. In Mark 11:1-15, we read about Jesus' triumphal entry into Jerusalem.

> And as they approached Jerusalem, at Bethphage and Bethany, near the Mount of Olives, He sent two of His disciples,
>
> and said to them, "Go into the village opposite you, and immediately as you enter it, you will find a colt tied there, on which no one yet has ever sat; untie it and bring it here.
>
> And if anyone says to you, "Why are you doing this?" you say, "The Lord has need of it"; and immediately he will send it back here.
>
> And they went away and found a colt tied at the door outside in the street; and they untied it.
>
> And some of the bystanders were saying to them, "What are you doing, untying the colt?"

And they spoke to them just as Jesus had told them, and they gave them permission.

And they brought the colt to Jesus and put their garments on it; and He sat upon it.

And many spread their garments in the road, and others spread leafy branches which they had cut from the fields.

And those who went before, and those who followed after, were crying out, "Hosanna! Blessed is He who comes in the name of the Lord;

Blessed is the coming kingdom of our father David; Hosanna in the highest!"

And He entered Jerusalem and came into the temple; and after looking all around, He departed for Bethany with the twelve, since it was already late.

And on the next day, when they had departed from Bethany, He became hungry.

And seeing at a distance a fig tree in leaf, He went to see if perhaps He would find anything on it; and when He came to it, He found nothing but leaves, for it was not the season for figs.

And He answered and said to it, "May no one ever eat fruit from you again!" And His disciples were listening.

And they came to Jerusalem. And He entered the temple and began to cast out those who were buying and selling in the temple, and overturned the tables of the moneychangers and the seats of those who were selling doves.

Scripture says that because of sin, the earth shall be cursed with **"thorns and thistles...and you shall eat the plants of the field; by the sweat of your face" (Genesis 3:17-19).** Anyone who has ever planted a garden or cultivated a yard knows that this is indeed true. The riddle of the painful earth, which many of us have been wrestling with for years, is the mystery that weeds grow faster than flowers. The riddle is also a mystery of walking in spiritual reality in the presence of futility and unreality.

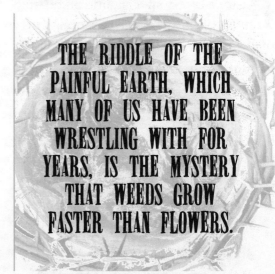

THE RIDDLE OF THE PAINFUL EARTH, WHICH MANY OF US HAVE BEEN WRESTLING WITH FOR YEARS, IS THE MYSTERY THAT WEEDS GROW FASTER THAN FLOWERS.

THE DREAM-BREAKER

A while back my wife was reading to me from a wonderful book called,

Love Stories God Told. One of the stories has a poem by William Butler Yeats entitled, *He Wishes for the Cloths of Heaven* that really impacted me:

> HAD I the heavens' embroidered cloths,
> Enwrought with the golden and silver light,
> The blue and the dim and the dark cloths
> Of night and light and half-light,
> I would spread the cloths under your feet
> But I, being poor, have only my dreams;
> I have spread my dreams beneath your feet;
> Tread softly because you tread on my dreams...

All my natural life I have sought to understand certain ineffable and unexplainable things of God in such a way that I could explain them to others. When my wife read those words, I saw something that I believe is a valuable and important insight for us individually, as a church, and as a nation. I saw by illumination Jesus as the "Dream-Breaker."

Just as the people in Jerusalem threw down their garments and palm branches for Jesus to walk over, we spread our dreams before Him and ask Him to tread upon them softly. The palm branches that they cut and laid under His feet are symbols of triumph and victory. The donkey on which no man had ever ridden symbolizes the kingdom coming to you in humility. The people waving their palm branches is a symbol of the

victory and triumph for which they had long sought.

As my wife read this poem, I saw that as the people waved their palm branches and threw them in front of Jesus as a symbol of their dream being realized, He was literally walking on their dreams. Everyone in Jerusalem, including the

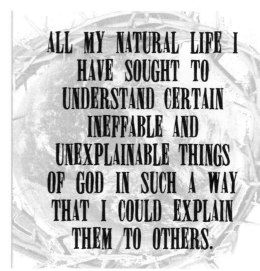

ALL MY NATURAL LIFE I HAVE SOUGHT TO UNDERSTAND CERTAIN INEFFABLE AND UNEXPLAINABLE THINGS OF GOD IN SUCH A WAY THAT I COULD EXPLAIN THEM TO OTHERS.

twelve disciples, honestly believed that in a few short weeks, or perhaps months, a literal kingdom would be re-established over all of Israel and they would be the lead nation in the earth. It is important to realize that their dreams were unreal and totally out of biblical perspective. Their false dreams persisted clear through the death and the resurrection of the Lord Jesus.

Even on the day of Pentecost they were still asking, **"Lord, is it at this time You are restoring the kingdom to Israel?" (Acts 1:6).** Their idea that there would be a literal kingdom had so captured their mind that Jesus answered and said, **"It is not for you to know times or epochs which the Father has fixed by His own authority"** (Acts 1:7). Sometimes our dreams are broken before He reveals the reality of His will.

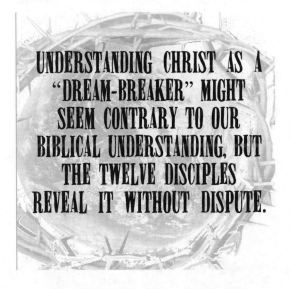

UNDERSTANDING CHRIST AS A "DREAM-BREAKER" MIGHT SEEM CONTRARY TO OUR BIBLICAL UNDERSTANDING, BUT THE TWELVE DISCIPLES REVEAL IT WITHOUT DISPUTE.

Chronologically, April 2 was the triumphal entry. On April 3, Jesus did two of the most significant things in His entire ministry—He cursed the fig tree and cleaned out the temple. Other than Jesus, no one, including the twelve disciples, understood what was happening.

The fig tree represents everything in our life which offers us false promises. This can involve all kinds of dreams and personal prophecy, as well as promises that have gone unfulfilled. This biblical parable is a riddle or a mystery of why Jesus must walk on our dreams when the dreams are not what the Lord wants for us at that time (even though they may be good things).

Cleansing the temple represents our lives getting so filled up with false dreams and empty promises, keeping us from all that God wants for our lives, that Jesus must clean things out. It is not an easy thing to endure and can even be violent at times. Unfortunately, we don't always understand what He's doing in our lives.

What Christ, who is Truth, had in mind was so different from what anyone understood, that He could not even explain it. He simply said, **"I have many more things to say to you, but you cannot bear them now"** (John 16:12). Can you see in His explanation the reservation He holds to walk on our dreams for our own benefit in order to fulfill God's purposes?

As Jesus entered the city, everyone was sure that a literal kingdom was going to appear at any moment. When the people asked Jesus if He was going to restore the literal kingdom to Israel, it was as if the dream itself had become a prison from which they could not possibly escape. All He could do was to break their false dreams and fulfill the Scriptures that involved the spiritual kingdom (see John 18:36).

Understanding Christ as a "Dream-Breaker" might seem contrary to our biblical understanding, but the twelve disciples revealed it without dispute.

From that time Jesus Christ began to show His disciples that He must go to Jerusalem, and suffer many things from the elders and chief priests and scribes, and be killed, and be raised up on the third day.

And Peter took Him aside and began to rebuke Him, saying, "God forbid it, Lord! This shall never happen to You."

But He turned and said to Peter, "Get behind Me, Satan! You are a stumbling block to Me; for you are not setting your mind on God's interests, but man's."

Then Jesus said to His disciples, "If anyone wishes to come after Me, let him deny himself, and take up his cross, and follow Me (Matthew 16:21-24).

The purpose of Christ's coming as a "Dream-Breaker" is to wean us from our own interests and relate us to God's interests. Since 1963, I have been pursuing the kingdom. It is not possible to count how many times I've had my own dreams walked upon in these many years. Over the weeks I was developing this theme, I remembered various dreams that Jesus was required to walk on and break in order for me to understand the reality of Him and His kingdom. Most of these dreams are now painful memories. No doubt, you've had your share as well. Many of us, consciously or unconsciously, have committed our life to dreams which were false or unreal. No one can be disillusioned until we first have an illusion, i.e. we have held to that which is untrue or false.

LYING AGAINST THE TRUTH

It is important to understand that holding to the dream itself may cause us to **"lie against the truth" (James 3:14).** We become so committed to our own dream and our understanding of what we think ought to happen that we are incapable of seeing God's purpose as it unfolds before us. A dream can become very fixed in our mind.

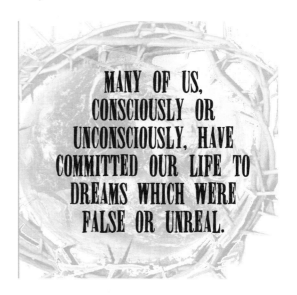

MANY OF US, CONSCIOUSLY OR UNCONSCIOUSLY, HAVE COMMITTED OUR LIFE TO DREAMS WHICH WERE FALSE OR UNREAL.

FUTILITY AND UNREALITY

I use God's mighty weapons, not those made by men, to knock down the devil's strongholds.

These weapons can break down every proud argument against God and every wall that can be built to keep men from finding him. With these weapons I can capture rebels and bring them back to God and change them into men whose hearts' desire is obedience to Christ (II Corinthians 10:4-5 TLB).

Jesus walking on our dreams is one of God's mighty weapons that is designed to break down the things we build which keep us from Him. With these weapons God can capture rebels, bring them back to Him, and change them into men whose hearts' desire is obedience to

Christ. A false dream is a prison of a most unusual kind. It keeps us from opening our inner person to God and His purpose. These dreams are doctrinal, devotional, self-referential, and conceptual. The Greek word for heresy is easily translated "a self-willed opinion." Which of us have not held some self-willed opinion about God, His purpose or the future that later we discovered was not only error, but also arrogant and totally misrepresented God?

> WHEN JESUS WALKED ON MY DREAMS IT WAS PAINFUL, AND CAUSED ME TO RE-EXAMINE THE RIDDLE OR MYSTERY OF HOW GOD'S WILL PREVAILED OVER OUR PERSONAL DESIRES.

A personal dream that I held onto for many years was to be a medical doctor or a surgeon. My deepest desire was to help people. The doctor under whom I trained used to ask for me to assist him in surgery. He offered to pay my way through college, medical school, and surgical internship. He would even pay my living expenses if I would agree to become a surgeon. It was a dream come true.

Needless to say Jesus walked on that dream. God spoke to me very directly, "You are a soul doctor called to mend and heal the spiritual needs of men and women." When Jesus walked on my dreams it was painful, and caused me to re-examine the riddle or mystery of how God's will prevailed over my personal desires. He had a call on my life for ministry and His dream must displace mine no matter what the cost.

The riddle of the painful earth can be seen in Romans 8 in the words **"futility"** and **"unreality."**

> **For the creation was subjected to *futility*, not of its own will, but because of Him who subjected it, in hope**
>
> **that the creation itself also will be set free from its slavery to *corruption* (Greek: *unreality*) into the freedom of the glory of the children of God (Romans 8:20-21).**

When I saw that **"creation itself"** was subjected to futility and unreality, it was like a freight train ran over me. I realized how committed we really can become to the **"futility"** and unreality of "good" dreams. It is evident that Western society is moving further and further away from reality. One family after another is being sold a "Disney World" dream of life and becomes disillusioned when those dreams are not realized. It is truly a curse on our society.

However, **"Christ redeemed us from the curse of the Law, having become a curse for us—for it is written, cursed is everyone who hangs on a tree" (Galatians 3:13).** He bore the thorns (symbolic of the curse) so that we could live in the **"freedom of the glory of the children of God."** God does not want us, as His people, to buy into the futility and the unreality that has so captured this world. He has dreams for us that may be different than what we had in mind.

MYSTERY

A mystery by its nature is ineffable—meaning it cannot be expressed or described in language or it is too great for words. God in action is a mystery. There is a mystery called original sin. Have you ever wondered why Christ doesn't annihilate all sin? Have you ever thought, "Well, Lord, why don't You just go out and get that bad guy and tie him up?" Have you ever said, "Lord, just *make* me obey! Don't knock, just tear the door off the hinges!" It is a mystery that the Lord does not, will not, coerce faith nor force our affection. It is a mystery how in the Person of Christ, deity and humanity were joined in hypostatic union. It is a mystery how Christ came to redeem and release us. It is a mystery that God designed freedom in such a way that it requires struggle.

It is also a mystery that because of futility and unreality, Christ is resisted from being formed in us. It is also a mystery that, as He pulls us out of our dream and gives us His dream, the likeness of Christ is worked into us and His nature becomes ours. He **"gave Himself for our sins, that He might deliver us out of this present evil age, according to the will of our God and Father" (Galatians 1:4).**

There is an important mystery behind Jesus' meaning of the triumphal entry into Jerusalem. God had more in mind than could be expressed in words. As Jesus entered Jerusalem, He saw things which transcended the literal city of Jerusalem. He saw a spiritual kingdom that reached the hurting in the nations of the world. His dream was that we would **"go therefore and make disciples of all the nations, baptizing them in the name of the Father and the Son and the Holy Spirit" (Matthew. 28:19).** He had something in mind that the disciples could not fathom.

THE RIDDLE OF THE PAINFUL EARTH IS THE BREAKING IN OF SPIRITUAL REALITY IN THE PRESENCE OF FUTILITY AND UNREALITY.

Because of the influence of futility and unreality, many times our own dreams are limited, restricted, and provincial. Illusion is what causes us to become disillusioned. No one can be disillusioned until they first have an illusion. The riddle of the painful earth is the breaking in of spiritual reality in the presence of futility and unreality. We have said many times "truth is always negative in its first appearance." This is often the case when our dreams are not what God wants for us.

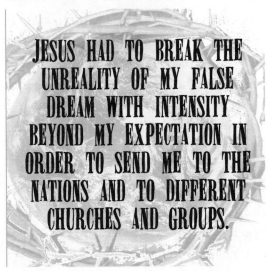

JESUS HAD TO BREAK THE UNREALITY OF MY FALSE DREAM WITH INTENSITY BEYOND MY EXPECTATION IN ORDER TO SEND ME TO THE NATIONS AND TO DIFFERENT CHURCHES AND GROUPS.

APPLICATION

The popular worship song, *Lord, Reign in Me,* speaks directly to having our dreams come into subjection to the will and purposes of God:

Over all the earth, You reign on high
Every mountain stream, every sunset sky
But my one request, Lord, my only aim
Is that You'd reign in me again

Lord, reign in me, reign in Your power
Over all my dreams, in my darkest hour
You are the Lord of all I am
So won't You reign in me again

Over every thought, over every word
May my life reflect the beauty of my Lord
'Cause You mean more to me than any earthly thing
So won't You reign in me again.

There have been many times for me personally when God walked on my dreams in order to impart His own. I wish I could have understood then what I am trying to say to you now. It would have made those difficult times much easier. False dreams caused the pain of a thousand changes because I thought the dreams were reality.

When Jesus was going up to be crucified He turned to the people and said, **"Daughters of Jerusalem, stop weeping for Me, but weep for yourselves and for your children" (Luke 23:28).** He knew what they could not know. He was aware of what was about to unfold upon Jerusalem, uprooting and refocusing everything they had ever understood.

There are many young men and women whose single dream is to be a millionaire before they are thirty-five years old. If God wants you to be a millionaire, that's wonderful, but some people will step on anyone who gets in the way of the fulfillment of their dream. The only thing more frightening than having Jesus walk on our dreams is to actually attain the false dream.

There was one false dream which I held onto with such tenacity that the dream itself held me in a prison from which I could not escape. I wish I could explain how stubborn I really was and how committed I was to my own dream. Jesus had to break the unreality of my false dream with intensity beyond my expectation in order to send me to the nations and to different churches and groups. The dream was my idea, not His. I did not understand what He had in His mind for me.

When Jesus took the disciples up on the Mount of Transfiguration, Moses and Elijah appeared for the purpose of turning over their teaching offices to Christ. **"Then a cloud formed, overshadowing them, and a voice came out of the cloud, 'This is My beloved Son, listen to Him!'"** (Mark 9:7). What God was doing in Mark 9 was getting us ready for Mark 11—that is a change in our focus and object. The focus must not be on Moses, Elijah, or any other person; our focus must rest on the Person of our Lord Jesus Christ!

Have you ever felt resisted by God or thought He wasn't cooperating with you? Have you ever said: "Lord, now let me explain this to You..."? When our marriage, home, finances, or other things are not turning out the way we wanted them to, it is often an issue of God changing our focus from people and things to the Person of Christ.

A GANG OF UGLY FACTS

Most of us have had the hard, ugly facts of life break the beautiful theories to which we had been clinging. While I was standing in absolute frustration in the middle of one of those times the Lord said, "Easy, Bob, easy! What I want to do is break your dream so that I can give you Mine." Only as we put our hand in His, is He able to take us beyond our dreams into the reality of His kingdom. His kingdom requires us to surrender our right to be offended. **"And blessed is he who keeps from stumbling over Me"** (Matthew 11:6).

Many people hold to their dream because it makes them feel complete, lessening the need for the Person of Christ. They feel they are not broken so they don't need anyone to fix them. They mistakenly think they are in perfectly good shape, they know what they want and where they are going. That is humanism and the pressure of our whole society.

> WHEN OUR MARRIAGE, HOME, FINANCES, OR OTHER THINGS ARE NOT TURNING OUT THE WAY WE WANTED THEM TO, IT IS OFTEN AN ISSUE OF GOD CHANGING OUR FOCUS FROM PEOPLE AND THINGS TO THE PERSON OF CHRIST.

A friend of mine was in a very serious crisis and he kept looking for an answer from God. Finally in the middle of the crisis he got angry at God and said, "Lord, all I need You to say is 'Yes' or 'No'. Why don't You do that?" A few days later he went to a meeting and there was a lady one seat in front of him. This woman kept saying out loud, "Yes, Lord! Yes, Lord, yes Lord!" He was getting increasingly more irritated by her outbursts. He thought to himself: I wish she could be quiet so I could hear what is being said. And the Lord said to him, "I'm not speaking to you from up there, I'm speaking to you from here." He said in agreement, "Yes, Lord!"

Many of us have walked with the Lord long enough to know that sometimes His voice comes from the most unexpected places—maybe even our spouse!

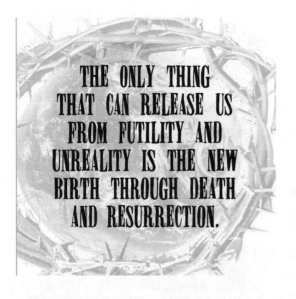

THE ONLY THING THAT CAN RELEASE US FROM FUTILITY AND UNREALITY IS THE NEW BIRTH THROUGH DEATH AND RESURRECTION.

SECOND EXODUS—THE NEW BIRTH

The first Exodus in the Old Testament was when God brought His people out of the bondage and futility of Egypt and carried them into the Promised Land. In the New Testament it is the Land of Promises.

The triumphal entry is the beginning of the second exodus—the new birth. Jesus entered my own city by the triumphal entry when I was a U.S. Navy sailor. I waved the palm branches and said, "Oh, Jesus has come!" Little did I know what kind of agenda He had in mind for me. Do you remember the freedom and joy you experienced when Jesus first came into your "city?" What we didn't know was how many false ideas and confused concepts we had which kept us imprisoned.

Understanding the new birth requires a kingdom world-view that is not complicated. There are three parts:

1. God is our Father and He *loves* us (see John 16:27).

2. *Nothing* touches our life except by His permission (see Matthew 10:29-31).

3. He redeems **"all things to work together for our good"** (Romans 8:28).

Even our false dreams can be redeemed. **"All things"** are like a mini-Gethsemane to us when the dreams that we have held onto go into death and resurrection. Only on resurrection day will we be able to see things differently. The reason we couldn't see clearly before is because futility and unreality held us in their iron grip. The only thing that can release us from futility and unreality is the new birth through death and resurrection.

SUMMARY

God is indeed breaking some dreams in Western civilization. When we throw our dreams before Him, allowing or even asking Him to walk on them, we need to know that He has a dream for us which is more than, other than, bigger than, we could possibly understand. As an emotionally injured, fighting sailor who drank straight vodka and was meaner than a junkyard dog, Jesus still came into my "city." As He enters our Jerusalem with His kingdom, He has one thing in mind—all the tribes, tongues, peoples, and nations of the world. He calls us up out of ourselves to be a voice to hurting people. He walks on our dreams for one all-encompassing reason—to impart His very own.

> Lord, reign in me, reign in Your power
> Over all my dreams, in my darkest hour
> You are the Lord of all I am
> So won't You reign in me again
>
> Over every thought, over every word
> May my life reflect the beauty of my Lord
> 'Cause You mean more to me than any earthly thing
> So won't You reign in me again.

Can you see this is a reckless prayer? If God reigns over all our dreams, we will be delivered from futility and unreality. He does this through the process of death and resurrection, bringing us into the sphere where He has washed our eyes with tears, allowing us to see things as they really are, as He sees them.

PRAYER

Father God, we need Your Son to enter our personal Jerusalem. We give You permission to walk on the dreams that are not from You. We desire to see with resurrection eyes and live in spiritual reality. Reign over all of our dreams. Through the reading of Your Word and the celebration of Your entrance into our "walled city," allow us to see into Your purposes in the earth. Lord, meet us where we are and bring us to resurrection and kingdom understanding for Jesus' sake. Amen. ■

Note: *Lord, Reign in Me* written by Brenton Brown, ©1998 Vineyard Songs (UK/Eire) (Admin. by Mercy / Vineyard Publishing) All rights reserved. International copyright secured. Used by permission. CCLI song #2490706. *Love Stories God Told*, written by David and Heather Kopp. Published by Harvest House, 1998.

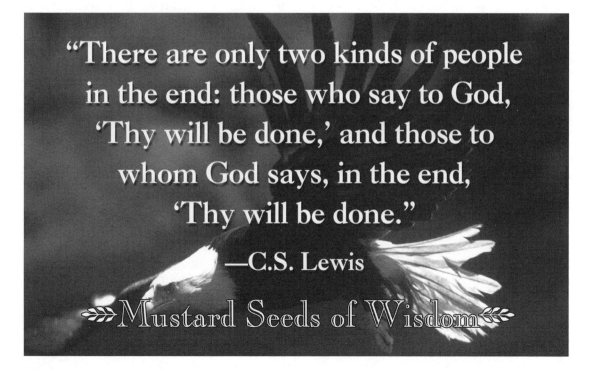

"There are only two kinds of people in the end: those who say to God, 'Thy will be done,' and those to whom God says, in the end, 'Thy will be done.'"

—C.S. Lewis

≫ Mustard Seeds of Wisdom ≪

CONFRONTING
THE ULTIMATE EVIL

by Rick Joyner

Basic to understanding the biblical prophecies of our time is the Lord's statement in Matthew 13:39, **"...the harvest is the end of the age..."** As He makes clear in His other parables and statements about the end of the age, this harvest is the reaping of everything that has been sown by man, both good and evil. Both are coming to full maturity, the righteous will become more righteous, and the wicked more wicked. Therefore, at the end of the age we will have the ultimate battle between good and evil.

It is for this reason that we must **"put on the full armor," (Ephesians 6:11)** given to us by God, and learn to use our divinely powerful weapons effectively. Two of the most powerful weapons that we have been given are love and truth. Therefore, a most

basic goal of our lives should be to walk in love and truth in all we do. As we are told in Romans 12:21: **Do not be overcome by evil, but overcome evil with good."**

Basically, we overcome every evil released on earth by growing in God's counter-power to it. We overcome the fear being released on the earth by walking in faith. We overcome the hatred and wrath by growing in love. We overcome rebellion and lawlessness by growing in obedience. In this way we discern the evil that is growing in the world and overcome it as we grow in God's grace, which counters it.

THE WISDOM OF THE HARVEST

In Matthew 13:30 the Lord sheds light on many of the things that are happening in our times. He is speaking here about the tares being sown in with the wheat:

> **"Allow both to grow together until the harvest; and in the time of harvest I will say to the reapers, "First gather up the tares and bind them in bundles to burn them up; but gather the wheat into my barn."**

We can see in the parable of the wheat and the tares a miniature history of the world. The Lord created a perfect earth for His children, and the devil came along and sowed tares in God's field. The Lord responded to this by telling His servants to let them both grow up, or mature, together. At the harvest, which is the end of the age, they will be separated. This separation is going on right now.

THE SEPARATION

We also need to understand that tares look like wheat, but are noxious. It is almost impossible to tell the two apart except at the harvest. They are easily distinguished at the harvest because the wheat begins to bow over, while the tares remain upright. We might say that with increasing maturity the wheat becomes more humble, and the tares become more arrogant.

I have talked to numerous people who have had dreams or visions of a sword coming which cuts off the head of everyone who is not bowing over. I think this is a prophetic picture of what is coming. Those bowed over are humble and devoted to prayer. Those standing upright

do not humble themselves, and are the tares who will be cut off.

Presently, there is most likely not a single church, ministry, or any other spiritual field that does not have tares mixed in with the wheat. As maturity comes, the distinctions will become more pronounced, and the separation accomplished.

> WE ALSO NEED TO UNDERSTAND THAT TARES LOOK LIKE WHEAT, BUT ARE NOXIOUS. IT IS ACTUALLY ALMOST IMPOSSIBLE TO TELL THE TWO APART EXCEPT AT THE HARVEST.

As we are told, we can expect the tares to start being gathered together into **"bundles."** It is noteworthy that in the parable the tares are gathered together first. I think we can see almost everywhere in the world that those who are prone to do evil have been gathering into organizations, groups, and even communities and nations. Presently, they are in more unity than the believers who are the **"wheat."** Even so, we are now in the time when the **"wheat,"** those who are born of the good seed, will be gathered together, coming into unprecedented unity.

Because of this unifying of evil in one group and the righteous in another, we are told in II Corinthians 6:14:

Do not be bound together with unbelievers; for what partnership have righteousness with lawlessness, or what fellowship has light with darkness?

The Lord does not want us to go out of the world, or He would have already taken us out. There are relationships we need and should have with unbelievers in order to be a witness to them. However, we do need to refrain from *covenant* relationships with unbelievers, which means to be **"bound together."** Those who are so **"bound together"** with unbelievers are going to be increasingly town between one camp or the other, and at some point, trying to live in both worlds will no longer be possible.

> IT IS FOR THIS REASON THAT THE DEATH AND DESTRUCTION WHICH COMES UPON THE WORLD AT THE END IS NOT SO MUCH THE RESULT OF GOD HURLING HIS JUDGEMENTS AT THE WORLD, AS IT IS THE CONSEQUENCES OF MAN'S OWN BEHAVIOR.

We must also be aware of the fact that unifying, for either good or evil, does increase power. As in the parable of the wheat and the tares, the evil is gathered into bundles first, and as stated, evil has in fact been unifying faster than the church until now. This is why evil has seemed more powerful, and has been advancing far more than the kingdom in many places. Even so, we are now coming to the time when the **"wheat"** will start gathering, coming into unity, and therefore growing in power. The tide of evil will be turned, which is already happening in many places.

THE ULTIMATE EVIL

The ultimate evil is rebellion against God. This is what released all death into the world in the first place, and it is basically what will cause all death and destruction in our times. The ultimate lesson, which all creation will learn from what comes upon the world at the end, is the consequences of thinking that we can do anything without God. Man was created to need God, and we do need Him. We will make a terrible mess of anything we do without Him.

It is for this reason that the death and destruction which comes upon the world at the end is not so much the result of God hurling His judgments at the world, as it is the consequences of man's own behavior. A basic spiritual principle is stated in Galatians 6:7:

Do not be deceived, God is not mocked; for whatever a man sows, this he will also reap.

Everyone will reap what they sow, so man will reap what he has sown. Much of the destruction that comes at the end is simply the consequence of man's own rebellion and determination to live without God.

The ultimate state of rebellion is known as **"lawlessness," (II Thessalonians 2:3)** which basically means to be without principles or moral code. This is precisely the state into which the wicked are coming. In contrast to this, the righteous will become more righteous. Their moral code will grow stronger and stronger, and so will their obedience to the Lord.

THE ULTIMATE EVIL PLAN, AND THE ULTIMATE WITNESS

Satan's ultimate purpose is to declare to the entire creation of God that man, the crown jewel of God's creation, loves Satan and his ways more than he loves God and His ways. Presently, Satan can point to the church and boast that even Christians love sin more than they love righteousness. This is why when a person remains obedient and faithful to God, by resisting the overwhelming temptations and pressures of this world to do evil, he becomes a witness to principalities and powers in the heavenly realm.

The bride of the first Adam lived in a perfect world, and yet chose to sin. The bride of the **"last Adam," (I Corinthians 15:45)** Christ, will live in the most imperfect world and against all of the power of evil in the darkest of times, and will choose to obey. For this reason all of creation will consider her worthy to reign with the King, Jesus.

Therefore, the ultimate test will be to live in obedience and faithfulness to God or fall into the ranks of lawlessness. Because love is the greatest force behind good, only those who truly love God will remain faithful. This is why the Lord stated in Matthew 24:12-13:

> **"And because lawlessness is increased, most people's love will grow cold.**
>
> **"But the one who endures to the end, he shall be saved.**

...WHEN A PERSON REMAINS OBEDIENT AND FAITHFUL TO GOD, BY RESISTING THE OVERWHELMING TEMPTATIONS AND PRESSURES OF THIS WORLD TO DO EVIL, HE BECOMES A WITNESS TO PRINCIPALITIES AND POWERS IN THE HEAVENLY REALM.

In II Corinthians 13:5 Paul said, **"Test yourselves to see if you are in the faith; examine yourselves!"** Possibly the most basic test to whether we are **"in the faith"** is if God is truly our first love. If He is, our primary goal in life will be to serve Him, please Him, and do His will.

The Lord said **"most people's love will grow cold,"** not just some. This should be a most sobering statement for any Christian. What will keep our love from growing cold? The Lord tells us in the same verse—**"lawlessness."** Therefore, one of the most important questions we can ask is: "Are we allowing our moral standards to erode along with the world's?" Which are we headed—toward the greater unity and obedience to the

Lord, or toward greater disobedience and lawlessness?

Some have been comforted by believing that it will be the heathen whose love will **"grow cold,"** but that is not accurate. The heathen do not even have a love for God in the first place. One thing we can know for sure about the end is that, because of lawlessness, the love of **"most"** Christians will **"grow cold."** Therefore, lawlessness is one of the ultimate tests which we can expect to try our hearts at the end.

> WHEN WE OPEN THE DOOR TO THE LUST OF THE FLESH, WHICH IS IMPURITY, WE OPEN THE DOOR WIDE TO LAWLESSNESS.

We must therefore be vigilant to watch over our hearts. Begin to ask now: "What is happening to our love?" If it is not getting stronger, it is getting weaker. Is our love for God being eroded because of lawlessness? We are told how this happens in Romans 6:19-23:

I am speaking in human terms because of the weakness of your flesh.

For just as you presented your members as slaves to impurity and to lawlessness,

resulting in further lawlessness, so now present your members as slaves to righteousness, resulting in sanctification.

For when you were slaves of sin, you were free in regard to righteousness.

Therefore what benefit were you then deriving from the things of which you are now ashamed? For the outcome of those things is death.

But now having been freed from sin and enslaved to God, you derive your benefit, resulting in sanctification, and the outcome, eternal life.

For the wages of sin is death, but the free gift of God is eternal life in Christ Jesus our Lord.

Here we see that impurity leads to lawlessness, and when we give ourselves to impurity, it leads to further lawlessness. I have actually heard people boast that they have never been unfaithful to their spouse, yet they are addicted to pornography. Did the Lord not say that, if a man even looks upon a woman to lust after her, he has committed adultery in his heart? (see Matthew 5:28) Even if we have not committed the physical act of adultery or fornication, it is impurity that leads to lawlessness.

When we open the door to the lust of the flesh, which is impurity, we open the door wide to lawlessness. When we do this, the first thing that becomes eroded is our love for God. Lust is actually the counter-power of true love, and therefore impurity makes true love start to grow cold very fast. As Paul exhorts in Galatians 5:16-25:

> But I say, walk by the Spirit, and you will not carry our the lust of the flesh.

> For the flesh sets its desires against the Spirit, and the Spirit against the flesh; for these are in opposition to one another, so that you may not do the things that you please.

> But if you are led by the Spirit, you are no under the law.

> Now the deeds of the flesh are evident, which are: immorality, impurity, sensuality,

> idolatry, sorcery, enmities, strife, jealousy, outbursts of anger, disputes, dissensions, factions,

> envying, drunkenness, carousing, and things like these, of which I forewarn you just as I have forewarned you that those who practice such things shall not inherit the kingdom of God.

> But the fruit of the Spirit is love, joy, peace, patience, kindness, goodness, faithfulness,

> gentleness, self-control; against such there is no law.

> Now those who belong to Christ Jesus have crucified the flesh with its passions and desires.

> If we live by the Spirit, let us also walk by the Spirit.

If we are not growing in the Spirit, which at least partly is accomplished by crucifying the flesh and its evil desires, we are going to be falling to those things which will ultimately cause the wrath of God to come. However, if our pursuit is to only not do the things that are evil, we will remain weak. What we must do is grow in God's counter-power to these things, As we are told in I John 3:3-4:

> LUST IS ACTUALLY THE COUNTER-POWER OF TRUE LOVE, AND THEREFORE IMPURITY MAKES TRUE LOVE START TO GROW COLD VERY FAST.

> And everyone who has this hope fixed on Him purifies himself, just as He is pure.

> Everyone who practices sin also practices lawlessness; and sin is lawlessness.

The greatest enemy of godliness, and the greatest power of destruction that is coming, will be released through lawlessness. The following are some of the Lord's statements about the consequences of giving ourselves to lawlessness:

"Many will say to Me on that day, 'Lord, Lord, did we not prophesy

in Your name, and in Your name cast out demons, and in your name perform many miracles?'

"And then I will declare to them, 'I never knew you; depart from Me, you who practice lawlessness.

ALL OF THE MINISTRIES AND GIFTS OF THE SPIRIT CAN GO ON WORKING IN OUR LIVES EVEN IF WE HAVE GIVEN OURSELVES OVER TO IMPURITY, IMMORALITY, OR ANY OTHER FORM OF LAWLESSNESS.

Could it be possible to **"practice lawlessness"** and still be able to prophesy, cast out demons, and even perform miracles in the Lord's name? Yes. As we are told in Romans 11:29 **"...the gifts and calling of God are irrevocable."** This means when the Lord gives something, He does not take it back, even if we become unfaithful. All of the ministries and gifts of the Spirit can go on working in our lives even if we have given ourselves over to impurity, immorality, or any other form of lawlessness. This is why we should discern His true servants by their fruit, not just their gifts.

In Matthew 13:41-42 the Lord says,

"The Son of Man will send forth His angels, and they will gather out

of His kingdom all stumbling blocks, and those who commit lawlessness,

and will cast them into the furnace of fire; in that place there will be weeping and gnashing of teeth.

Here we are told that the time is coming when the Lord will gather these **"stumbling blocks"** out of His kingdom, and without question, all who fall to lawlessness will become stumbling blocks. This is the last thing that we should ever want to be, because He warned in Luke 17:1-2:

"It is inevitable that stumbling blocks should come, but woe to him through whom they come!

"It would be better for him if a millstone were hung around his neck and he were thrown into the sea, than that he should cause one of these little ones to stumble."

In Matthew 23:27-28 we are given another important characteristic of lawlessness:

"Woe to you, scribes and Pharisees, hypocrites! For you are like whitewashed tombs which on the outside appear beautiful, but inside are full of dead men's bones and all uncleanness.

"Even so you too outwardly appear righteous to men, but inwardly you are full of hypocrisy and lawlessness."

We usually think of lawlessness as rebellion, the craftiness that is always trying to bend the rules and get away with it, or even anarchy. Here we see that those who were apparently the most given to keeping the law were **"full of hypocrisy and lawlessness."** Legalism is not the answer to lawlessness—it actually promotes lawlessness. It promotes cleaning up the externals so that we may appear righteous before men, but it actually leads to an even deeper corruption of the heart.

There have been many legalistic movements in the church who have tried to deliver men from lawlessness with legalism, or even the submission to what is in fact a control spirit. These things can change the behavior of some, but they can never change the heart, and it is the heart that God looks upon. The only thing that really changes our heart is love. Those who truly love God are devoted to doing that which pleases Him. Anything but love will eventually wither under the onslaught of lawlessness which is now being released in the world.

Therefore the ultimate goal should be, just what Paul said in I Timothy 1:5,

"But the goal of our instruction is love from a pure heart and a good conscience and a sincere faith."

There are many practical things we can do to guard our hearts from the onslaught of lawlessness. Simple things like obeying rules, regulations, and laws (which includes speed limits, paying taxes, etc.). We should start loving and appreciating these rules. Just imagine what this world would be like without them.

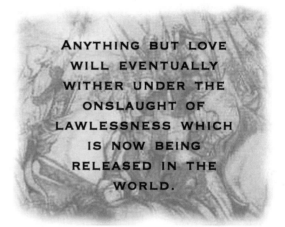

ANYTHING BUT LOVE WILL EVENTUALLY WITHER UNDER THE ONSLAUGHT OF LAWLESSNESS WHICH IS NOW BEING RELEASED IN THE WORLD.

THE HIGHEST HONOR

If we were told that the President of the United States, or a king, was coming to stay at our home for a week, how many of us would not have it looking better than it probably ever had before? We would not just clean, but we would scrub, we would paint, and we might even remodel. Some might even be prone to buy a new house! My point is that we have Someone much greater than the President living in us now—we have the Holy Spirit of God! How much more should we be trying to keep our house in order for Him? How could anyone who truly loves God not feel this way?

If we will love God, and love one another, we will stand against any evil that comes in the last days. ■

THE SUBTLETY OF COMPROMISE

by Mike Roberts

As Christians our primary purpose is to know the Lord and walk with Him. The very reason we were created is to have fellowship with God. For this reason the devil's schemes are always designed to distract us from the Lord. He does not care what replaces the Lord as the center of our attention, just as long as he can lure us from His presence. The devil is completely satisfied to let a small sin draw us away from the Lord, if that is all that is necessary.

Dangers of Lukewarmness

As a person is distracted and begins to compromise in his pursuit of the Lord, he can often become lukewarm. The Bible tells us that lukewarmness is a condition that the Lord will not tolerate in His people. Revelation 3:15-16 says:

> I know your deeds, that you are neither cold nor hot; I would that you were cold or hot.
>
> So because you are lukewarm, and neither hot nor cold, I will spit you out of My mouth.

It may seem surprising to us the Lord would say that He would rather His people be cold than lukewarm, but this is exactly what He said. Obviously, He wants us to be hot and not cold, but it is easier for the Lord to get the attention of an outright sinner than it is for Him to get through to a Christian living in a state of constant compromise. In the next verse of the same chapter, Jesus says:

> Because you say, "I am rich, and have become wealthy, and

have need of nothing," and you do not know that you are wretched and miserable and poor and blind and naked,

In this verse, the Lord is describing people who are considerably deceived. They believe that everything is great and could not possibly be better, but in reality they are in a very desperate state. One common misconception is that lukewarmness is when a person is hot one day and cold the next. However, lukewarmness does not result when a person shifts back and forth between being hot and cold, it results when they are neither hot nor cold. This is one reason lukewarmness can be hard to detect.

A Practical Illustration

Several years ago, I kept a few hermit crabs as pets, and the Lord taught me a lesson in lukewarmness through my care of them. Unlike some animals, crabs have gills, not lungs, and in order for them to be able to breathe properly, their gills must remain moist. To accomplish this, it is recommended that they be dipped in "lukewarm" water a few times a week.

Once while I was submerging one of the crabs into the water, it occurred to me that in order for the water to be lukewarm, it can be neither hot nor cold. It would not have been the same if they had been dipped into hot water one day and cold water the next. The only way to properly care for the crabs was to dip them in water, which had a temperature in the perfect range, having just the right amount of hot mixed with the right amount of cold. It is the same in our spiritual lives.

Lukewarmness develops as we become lax in our pursuit of the Lord, not when we abandon it altogether. Being hot one day and cold the next is certainly a sign of a problem, but it is a problem which is usually obvious. When we are lukewarm, we are often not even aware that there is a problem. Let us now look at how this subtle problem can develop.

When we are lukewarm, we are often not even aware that there is a problem.

How Does This Happen?

How does a Christian go from a place of being close to the Lord to a place where he does not even realize that he has begun to stray from His presence? As we have already discussed, the devil is satisfied to let even a small sin distract us from the Lord. He knows most Christians would never go from being hot to being cold overnight, so he will rarely even try to tempt us in this way. Instead, he will try to cause us to compromise little by little until, after a while, we have greatly wandered from the path of life.

If we are standing close to the Lord, the devil will never ask us to walk ten feet away from Him, but he will try to gently nudge us away six inches at a time. Once we have taken that initial six-inch step, it does not take very long before we are comfortable being six inches away from the Lord. Once we are comfortable there, the devil will nudge us another six inches. Finally we have gradually wandered much farther from the Lord than we ever would have at one time. This is when we have the problem. Once we are comfortable standing a few feet from the Lord, we do not even realize that there is any distance at all between us. Finally, we end up in the state described in the preceding verse, and we do not even know it.

> **None of us would ever want to settle for casual encounters with the Lord, but as our spiritual condition changes, so does our perception.**

Larry Randolph once said, "When we compromise our commitment to Christ, we are left with nothing more than casual encounters with the Spirit of God." None of us would ever want to settle for casual encounters with the Lord, but as our spiritual condition changes, so does our perception. Before long we actually begin to believe that the casual encounters are really not casual at all, but profound. If we are in this state, we often resist the Lord's prompting and become like those described in Revelation 3:17. This is why the Lord would rather that we be cold. When we are lukewarm, we begin to believe that we are **"rich, and have become wealthy, and have need of nothing,"** when we are really **"wretched and miserable and poor and blind and naked."**

Is There a Remedy?

Certainly lukewarmness is one of the worst states in which we could possibly find ourselves. Even though it can be difficult to discern, the Holy Spirit can identify this condition in our lives, lead us out of it, and restore us back to the Lord. Let us look again in Revelation 3. In verses 18 and 19, once Jesus has identified the lukewarmness, He offers a solution:

> **I advise you to buy from Me gold refined by fire, that you may become rich, and white garments, that you may clothe yourself, and that the shame of your nakedness may not be revealed; and eye salve to anoint your eyes, that you may see.**

> **Those whom I love, I reprove and discipline; be zealous therefore, and repent.**

The Lord promises here that He really will make into reality what we previously just thought was reality. He advises us to buy from Him refined gold that we **"may become rich"** and white garments that our nakedness will be covered. He will take us from a place of believing that we have everything, but actually having nothing, to truly being in need of nothing. We are only in need of nothing when we are with the Lord. He commands us to **"be zealous therefore, and repent."** Through repentance, we change our thinking and our direction. Hebrews 4:12 says:

For the word of God is living and active and sharper than any two-edged sword, and piercing as far as the division of soul and spirit, of both joints and marrow, and able to judge the thoughts and intentions of the heart.

Jeremiah 23:29 says:

"Is not my word like fire?" declares the Lord...

The Word of God not only exposes what is in our hearts, but it also cleanses and purifies us. It is as we draw close to the Lord and take His Word inside us that we are changed, and the fire of His presence leaves us hot and dispels any lukewarmness in our lives.

Guarding Our Hearts

As we have seen, the enemy is very subtle in his attempts to get us to compromise. If he can get us to deviate from the path of life and away from the presence of the Lord, a condition of lukewarmness can develop in our lives. In order to guard against this condition, we must constantly keep watch over our hearts. Proverbs 4:23 says:

Watch over your hearts with all diligence, for from it flow the springs of life.

Whatever we take into our hearts is what will be manifested in our lives. If we compromise with what we allow into our hearts, it will result in a distance growing between the Lord and us. If we are going to know the Lord and walk with Him the way in which He intends, we cannot leave

any room in our lives for compromise. A person who is lukewarm believes he is in need of nothing, but we are constantly in need of the Lord. We are completely dependent upon the Lord for our very lives, and His supernatural power and grace make it possible for us to live a life of holiness. As we make a fresh connection with the Spirit of the Lord every day, we keep our faith fresh and receive His grace and power, enabling us to live our lives in passionate pursuit of the Lord, and live above lukewarm Christianity.

> It is as we draw close to the Lord and take His Word inside us that we are changed, and the fire of His presence leaves us hot and dispels any lukewarmness.

Seeing that His divine power has granted to us everything pertaining to life and godliness, through the true knowledge of Him who called us by His own glory and excellence.

For by these He has granted to us His precious and magnificent promises, in order that by them you might become partakers of the divine nature, having escaped the corruption that is in the world by lust (II Peter 1:3-4). ∎

Awake to Righteousness

by Deborah Joyner Johnson

"Awake to righteousness, and sin not" (I Corinthians 15:34 KJV).

Have we actually been asleep to righteousness, as the above Scripture states? Looking at the world, one could definitely come to this conclusion, as many are slumbering in sin because their senses are dulled as to what is right and wrong.

The question arises: Have some Christians fallen into this snare of indifference? We need to seriously ponder this in our own hearts. The enemy will set a trap to capture those who seek after their own pleasures, which is all too easy to fall into if seeking the Lord wholeheartedly is not our priority. Being righteous should set us apart from those who are of the world. We are called to be lights—not caught in the darkness that controls those who do not know the Lord.

To understand what it means to be righteous, let us look at just a few of the thirty-six attributes in a thesaurus. Righteous means to be: honorable, goodhearted, noble, moral, honest, trustworthy, guiltless, blameless, and having a clear conscience. How do we measure up to this definition?

Basically, if we are righteous, we are pure and do not sin. Can we truly be pure in our world today? It is a high calling, but Jesus is our standard of righteousness. If we will aspire to become like Jesus, then we will eventually become righteous. As we can conclude from the above Scripture, we are instructed to awaken from our slumber, and to be just that—righteous.

Righteous vs. Religious

There is quite a difference between being righteous and being religious. The scribes and Pharisees had the appearance of being righteous, religiously doing good works, but on the inside, they were full of pride. The most stern language that Jesus ever used in the Bible was when He talked to the scribes and Pharisees, speaking seven woes against them. Here is just one:

"Woe to you, scribes and Pharisees, hypocrites! For you clean the outside of the cup and of the dish, but inside they are full of robbery and self-indulgence.

You blind Pharisee, first clean the inside of the cup and of the dish, so that the outside of it may become clean also" (Matthew 23:25-26).

This truth is hard to hear, but God placed it in the Bible for a purpose and for us to learn from. The Pharisees were the epitome of the religious spirit. They made sure that they "appeared" righteous, but Jesus could see their hearts, and they were anything but righteous, as their hearts were full of pride.

The world, which so desperately needs Jesus, picks up on the legalism that follows the religious spirit, which turns them completely from the Lord. This is why the Lord spoke so harshly to the scribes and Pharisees because He knew what they were doing to the lost. Jesus came to save the lost, and they were turning many from following God, thinking they were doing Him a favor by persecuting those who did not live up the their "holier than thou" standard.

Jesus said: **"...unless your righteousness surpasses that of the scribes and Pharisees, you shall not enter the kingdom of heaven" (Matthew 5:20).** Jesus gave this warning to us as well. It may seem like we are a far cry from being anything like a Pharisee, but we may need to think about that again. Let us pray and ask God to remove pride from our lives and help us become righteous, as He is. He will help us.

> New Christians are not changed overnight and they will still have many of their old ways, as we all did when we first came to the Lord.

Sobering Truth

I was recently told the following story and it broke my heart. A young lady had just met the Lord. She was having a few drinks, and a Christian began berating her for drinking—telling her it was a terrible thing to do. She felt condemned, guilty, and rejected. Her thoughts were: "Why even bother trying to be a Christian—I can't do it!" It is likely that this young woman had not even been a Christian long enough to learn that some of the things she was doing were wrong. Sadly, the harshness with which her behavior was confronted did not encourage her toward righteousness, but discouraged her.

New Christians are not changed overnight and they will still have many of their old ways, as we all did when we first came to the Lord. We may have a tendency to immediately try to "fix" someone when they first become saved, but we should not be the Holy Spirit to others. Which one of us became perfect overnight? It takes time for healing and the Lord to change new followers into His image. So we must have patience with others.

We can correct someone about a matter that is in fact true, and yet do it in a wrong spirit, causing wounds instead of the liberty that comes from the truth of God, which sets us free. Furthermore, wounds can be very deep and the person who is being healed has to want to be healed. But with time, as they seek the Lord and develop their own relationship with Him, they will become more like Him and be changed into His image. We must always remember, it is God who will do the changing, not us.

> When someone is going through a process of healing, the last thing they need to hear is condemnation from anyone.

Choice Words Follow the Righteous

The situation with the young Christian woman could have been so different if she had heard encouraging words, instead of condemning words. Proverbs 10:20 states: **"The tongue of the righteous is as choice silver, the heart of the wicked is worth little."** We would all like to take back things that we have said, so it is very important to be careful with our words to begin with. We want our words to be **"as choice silver,"** but this takes the practice of self-control and prayer. You see, being righteous comes from the outgrowth of our relationship with God.

As we become more like Jesus, our words will become like His.

The Heart of Jesus

Jesus had many friends, and most lived questionable lives. Why did they want to be with Him? Because they felt accepted by Him; He loved them and it showed. He came with open arms to those who were not accepted by the so-called "religious" of their society, the scribes and Pharisees. Neither was Jesus accepted by these same religious ones, but was rather delivered up to be crucified by them.

Jesus came to save the brokenhearted, having great compassion for them. **The LORD is near to the brokenhearted, and saves those who are crushed in spirit (Psalm 34:18).** He is our example of righteousness and we should likewise help those who are crushed in spirit. My heart goes out to that young lady who so recently met the Lord. She too may have been **"brokenhearted"** or **"crushed in spirit."** Who knows the reason why she was drinking too much? We do not know her past or her heart. Perhaps she had been addicted to cocaine, and she was trying desperately not to get a fix, so she drank instead. Those who are addicted, or have been addicted to drugs, know that it is difficult to stop. Instead of condemnation, she needed someone to accept her just the way she was. She needed a friend to love her through her problems.

When someone is going through a process of healing, the last thing they need to hear is condemnation from anyone. They have enough condemnation and guilt from the enemy, without others heaping coals on top of that. The Holy Spirit is the One who does the convicting. We must pray for that person, leave it with the Lord, and just be a friend. Remember: **"Above all, love each other deeply, because love covers over a multitude of sins (I Peter 4:8 NIV).**

If we are becoming righteous, then we are taking on the nature of Christ. When we truly love the Lord and know that He loves us, that love will shine forth from us as an extension of our relationship with Him, and then it will be given to others. This is the essence of being righteous.

Just Accept

What keeps those who may not "look" like Christians out of the churches? Most of the time it is guilt and condemnation from the church. Maybe some have ten tattoos and two nose rings. God loves them just as they are and we should too. Why does it matter anyway? God looks at the heart, not the outside, which should be our example to love others as well. As we grow in His love, becoming more righteous, we will begin to love those around us.

What about a homeless person? They need compassion, not condemnation. Those just getting out of prison need friends to surround them. They may have met the Lord there, but when they return to society, it is all too easy to fall back into sin. I Corinthians 15:33 states: **"Do not be deceived: 'Bad company corrupts good morals.'"** If they aren't accepted in the church, where else are they going to go? Sadly, they will go back to where they are accepted, to their old friends and old ways. We can make a difference in this world—we can love the unlovable through the power of His love.

We are called to be **"the light of the world. A city set on a hill cannot be hidden. Nor do men light a lamp, and put it under the peck measure, but on the lampstand; and it gives light to all who are in the house. Let your light shine before men…" (Matthew 5:14-16).**

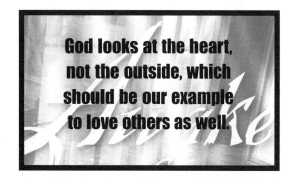

God looks at the heart, not the outside, which should be our example to love others as well.

How can we awake to righteousness and make a difference? By letting our lights shine in a dark world that has no hope. Accept and love those who may be unacceptable in the eyes of many, just as Jesus in His life on earth gave us as an example. The world is a sad and lonely place. The unsaved and the hurting need the Lord, the brightest Light of all. May we learn to be compassionate, just as Jesus cares for us.

Light arises in the darkness for the upright; He is gracious and compassionate and righteous (Psalm 112:4).

One Christian is just a single light, but it is still a light and many can be drawn to the Light within you. But if we all shine together, the world will become a brighter place. Proverbs 4:18 states: **"But the path of the righteous is like the light of dawn, that shines brighter and brighter until the full day."** As we individually become more like Jesus, corporately we will become the righteous lights the Lord has called us to be. And, we will make a difference. ∎

CHILD OF GOD

THEOLOGY VS. REALITY

All Scriptures are New International Version unless otherwise indicated.

by Hombre Liggett

We are dwelling in a time when living what we actually believe is rare. God is causing believers to become more aware of the vast difference between believing in His truths and walking in those truths through faith in Christ. Recently, I came across a passage in which God began to speak to me concerning this very issue.

Salvation—a Bridge to God's Eternal Purposes

Before going further let us emphasize some facts regarding our salvation. (It will become more obvious later why we are spending the time to do this). Romans 10:9 makes it clear that any person who will confess with their mouth and believe

in their heart the Lordship and resurrection of Jesus Christ will be saved. We know speaking the words "Jesus is Lord" is not a magic formula. Confessing with our mouth must mean more than just moving our lips to speak these words. It speaks more of a life confession than just the willingness to say something. The fact is that even demons believe in Jesus, and they know that He is Lord, and yet are not saved.

We need to be sure we are not confessing Christ in one environment, but then producing lives that deny Him to the multitudes. Scripture tells us if we confess Jesus Christ before men, Jesus will then confess us before the Father, and if we deny Him then He will do the same concerning us to the Father (see Matthew 10:32-33). God is concerned with how we live among people, and not just what we say around others. Therefore, our testimony is more weighted by how we live with the understanding that our good behavior will never get us into heaven.

The conclusion of our salvation is determined by our faith, but James tells us that **"faith without works is dead" (James 2:20 NKJV).** Still, even if all our works are temporal rather than eternal, we still will be saved, but just barely (see I Corinthians 3:10-15).

With that established in our understanding, we turn to a deeper subject than our salvation in and of itself. Jesus did not die on the cross for the sole purpose of getting us out of hell. Our salvation has a much greater purpose than that. We must remove ourselves from seeing the cross only as a "fire escape," and see it as a bridge to God's eternal purposes for us.

> **"He was in the world, and though the world was made through Him, the world did not recognize Him.**
>
> **He came to that which was His own, but His own did not receive Him.**
>
> **Yet to all who received Him, to those who believed in His name, He gave the *right* to become children of God" (John 1:10-12 NIV).**

J. B. Phillips (New Testament in Modern English) translates verse 12, **"yet wherever men did accept Him, He gave them the *power* to become sons of God."**

We Are a New Creation

As we believe in God and are born-again, we are cleansed of our sins. We become vessels of God's Spirit. A glorious process begins in our lives of being sanctified by the power of the Spirit of God, and being transformed into the image of Christ. How far this process goes is up to us and not the Lord.

We must remove ourselves from seeing the cross only as a "fire escape," and see it as a bridge to God's eternal purposes for us.

All Christians are God's children **"You are all sons of God through faith in Christ Jesus" (Galatians 3:26),** but not all Christians live according to the advantages, authority, and power which comes with being a child of the living God. To every person who has believed upon the name of Jesus, God has given the *ability* to become His son or daughter, in operation and not just in theory. God has given to every Christian the "power" to be a functional child of His (see John 1:12 KJV). This would imply that as followers of Christ the fulfillment of actually living as God's sons and daughters is in our own hands.

Our beliefs about being a child of the King tend to rest more in our theology than in our reality. To each who has put their faith in Christ, the ability and power have been given to live under the rights of being a child of God. God does not want us just associated with Him. By the blood of Jesus He is adopting children and wants those sons and daughters to live up to the family name by walking under its authority.

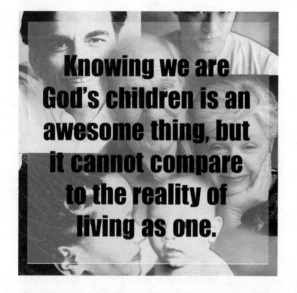

Knowing we are God's children is an awesome thing, but it cannot compare to the reality of living as one.

Another passage which needs time of its own to fully explore is found in I Peter 1:23. **"For you have been born again not of seed which is perishable but imperishable, that is, through the living and abiding word of God.** Just think: a life conceived by God Himself! Here it suggests that our new birth is actually a new creation, a new species created by God. If we are conceived in life by mortal sperm, then here it hints that God has given conception and birth again to us through His Spirit. The Holy Spirit conceived God's Son Jesus, and

God has ordained us to be like Him. The only way we can be His children is through spiritual conception and birth. If we are going to live in the reality of this new birth as God's children, then it must be done through the Spirit. Living by the Spirit is not what we just believe, but it is what we must do.

A close friend of mine, who is a gifted teacher in the church, shared recently that there is a difference between our legal position in Christ and our experiential position with Christ. Legally, we are crucified with Christ and are seated with Him upon the throne, but experientially most are still trying to die to self and walk under the authority of Christ. We know by faith the legal part is truth, but we are hard-pressed to produce the results in our lives to prove it.

Legally, we are children of God. God wants us to operate as His children, and not just claim to be one. When confronted by those standing only by their legal claim to be children of Abraham, John the Baptist declared that out of stones God could raise up children of Abraham (see Matthew 3:9). Knowing our legal position in Christ is of little use to His kingdom until we accept the responsibility of such truths and then strive to live accordingly.

Knowing we are God's children is an awesome thing, but it cannot compare to the reality of living as one. Living as His child is not about attitude but about purpose. It is about doing His will in building His kingdom. God is sending His sons and daughters as His true ambassadors into the world to represent Him. The ambassadors of God's kingdom are not just His children by legality, but they are those who are functionally His offspring.

Hearing the Voice of God

The difference between being a legal son through faith in Christ, and operating as one, is determined by being led by God's Spirit. **"All who follow the leading of God's Spirit are God's own sons" (Romans 8:14 J.B. Phillips).** We may have the Holy Spirit living inside of us, but that is a far cry from being led by God's Spirit. The presence of the Holy Spirit in us only gives us the grand privilege of being led by God, but it does not make it automatic.

The ability to be led by the Spirit of God is determined by being able to hear the voice of God. Jesus said that His sheep know His voice, and they follow the voice of no other (see John 10:4-5). Legally all who are born-again are children of God, but there is this existence within God's offspring to which He refers directly. To those who hear and obey His voice, He identifies more specifically as His children, yet not in a legal sense but in an intimate and powerful way.

> **"The man who is born of God can hear these words of God and the reason why you can not hear the words of God is simply this, that you are not the sons of God" (John 8:47 J. B. Phillips).**

Do we need to actually hear the **"words of God"** to be a child of God? As determined earlier, our salvation is through faith in Christ alone. As hard as it might be to accept by some, God has an elite force of people inside the church family. These "special forces" are made up of those who not only believe the truth, but also strive daily to live it through knowing and listening to the voice of God.

God desires for the church to move in her legal positions in Christ, not just claim them. In America we have the right to freedom, free enterprise, and to pursue happiness. Those rights are only fully beneficial if we exercise and function in them.

The presence of the Holy Spirit in us only gives us the grand privilege of being led by God, but it does not make it automatic.

We should never abandon what has been legally established for us. The functionality of legal position is not just knowing our rights but exercising them. How do we do this? The answer is simplistic. Sensitivity to God's voice is acquired by getting close to Him. There are no shortcuts. This message is not something we read and then go away saying, "I'm just going to start boldly acting as a child of God." Living as a child of God is not something we act out like a Thespian. It requires knowing the Lord and being close to Him. This will not result from textbook understanding, but it is an intimate communion with Christ. We must hear His voice. Those currently hearing God's voice must grow closer to Him and hear more clearly. God always wants us closer to Him. He will often even grow seemingly quieter as you get closer. He does this to draw you even nearer to Himself.

We need to lay hold of what God "legally" made available to us. The cross of Christ is a pathway to entering the kingdom of God and not just escaping hell. Our position in the kingdom is determined by our relationship to God and being led by His Spirit.

People often ask: Who will be seated close to Christ in His kingdom? The answer is simply those who are close to Him *now* are those who will be close to Him *then*. We do not earn the right to be close to Him just by the works we do. Our ultimate kingdom status is determined by where we are relationally to Him through this life on earth. Any good child of God does the will of the Father and is given a place in His house.

Initiating our legal position in Christ should bring us to an experiential place of relationship with God. Today is the day and now is the time. We can't let our hearts be hardened to God's voice as in the days of the rebellion (see Hebrews 3:7-8). God's cry is: "Come close to Me, My sons and My daughters, and be Mine, for I have created for you from the beginning for good works to do in My Name!"

Abba, Father! ■

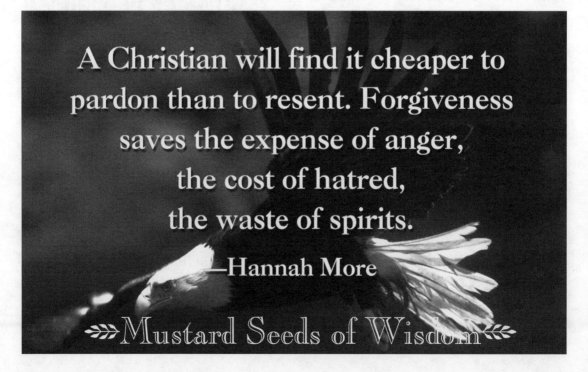

A Christian will find it cheaper to pardon than to resent. Forgiveness saves the expense of anger, the cost of hatred, the waste of spirits.

—Hannah More

≫≫ Mustard Seeds of Wisdom ≪≪

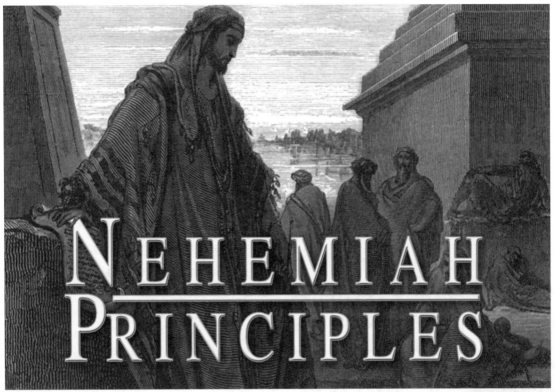

NEHEMIAH PRINCIPLES

by Cary Summers

The following are a list of leadership qualities that we can draw from just one book of the Bible. Consider them:

1. Great leaders have concern for the condition of others (Nehemiah 1:1-2).

2. Great leaders have the ability to listen (Nehemiah 1:3).

3. Great leaders not only have a concern for others, but they also have compassion (Nehemiah 1:4).

4. Great leaders understand the needs of others (Nehemiah 1:4).

5. Great leaders do not rush to a conclusion (Nehemiah 1:4).

6. Great leaders rely upon God and recognize God's power (Nehemiah 1:5).

7. Great leaders not only pray but they also make themselves available to meet the need (Nehemiah 1: 6-11).

8. Great leaders do not run ahead of God. Praying and waiting go hand in hand (Nehemiah 2:1).

9. Great leaders understand that God specializes in changing the hearts of leaders (Nehemiah 2:1).

10. Great leaders have the ability to handle difficult situations and still show respect for their superiors (Nehemiah 2:3).

11. Great leaders admit their human weaknesses (Nehemiah 2:3).

12. Great leaders consider the other person's point of view before responding (Nehemiah 2:3).

13. Great leaders know how to depend upon God and to allow God to speak through them (Nehemiah 2:4).

14. Great leaders do not use faith as a substitute for required, careful planning (Nehemiah 2:5).

15. Great leaders spend most of their time in strategic issues, not fire drills (Nehemiah 2:5).

16. Great leaders go through proper channels (Nehemiah 2:8).

17. Great leaders who walk by faith will be opposed by those who walk by sight (Nehemiah 2:10).

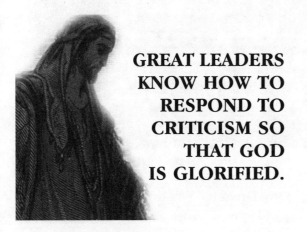

GREAT LEADERS KNOW HOW TO RESPOND TO CRITICISM SO THAT GOD IS GLORIFIED.

18. Great leaders know how to handle themselves in solitude—in silence (Nehemiah 2:11).

19. Great leaders know how to pick people who can be trusted (Nehemiah 2:12).

20. Great leaders develop patience in allowing God to lead (Nehemiah 2:12).

21. Great leaders spend the necessary time to formulate the plan that God can endorse (Nehemiah 2:13-15).

22. Great leaders identify with the people and the need (Nehemiah 2:17-18).

23. Great leaders explain the situation, stick to the facts, explain the plan, and touch the hearts of the people (Nehemiah 2:17-18).

24. Great leaders allow God to use them to turn despair into hope (Nehemiah 2:17-18).

25. Great leaders know how to handle criticism (Nehemiah 2:19).

26. Great leaders know how to use the authority of their position (Nehemiah 2:20).

27. Great leaders know how to coordinate efforts (Nehemiah 3).

28. Great leaders know how to gain cooperation (Nehemiah 3).

29. Great leaders are encouragers (Nehemiah 3).

30. Great leaders know how to respond to criticism so that God is glorified. They give the opposition over to God (Nehemiah 4:4-5).

31. Great leaders work and pray (Nehemiah 4:6).

32. Great leaders know how to lead the troops through the difficult times and keep up morale (Nehemiah 4:6).

33. Great leaders address the issue head on and take action (Nehemiah 4:13).

34. Great leaders unify the trips around a common objective (Nehemiah 4:14).

35. Great leaders do not allow stress and discouragement to derail them from the vision (Nehemiah 4:14).

36. Great leaders, in time of stress and discouragement, focus their eyes upon the God of all power rather than on the discouragement (Nehemiah 4:14).

37. Great leaders help the balance (Nehemiah 4:14).

38. Great leaders provide a strategy for people to rally around (Nehemiah 4:19-20).

39. Great leaders serve others (Nehemiah 4:21-23).

40. Great leaders carefully deliberate before taking action (Nehemiah 5:7).

41. Great leaders confront even the nobles when human dignity is being exploited (Nehemiah 5:7).

42. Great leaders do what is right even when doing it is costly (Nehemiah 5:7).

43. Great leaders exemplify in their own life what they expect of others (Nehemiah 5:10).

44. Great leaders not only expose the problem, but they also provide a solution (Nehemiah 5:10).

45. Great leaders know how to balance power and privilege so that God is glorified (Nehemiah 5:14).

46. Great leaders know how to relinquish their rights (Nehemiah 5:14).

47. Great leaders understand integrity and exercise it in their daily dealings (Nehemiah 5:15).

48. Great leaders consciously work at keeping themselves above reproach (Nehemiah 5:16).

49. Great leaders show their true character in times of crisis (Nehemiah 5:19).

50. Great leaders know how to ask great questions, especially in times of great pressure (Nehemiah 6:3).

51. Great leaders know how to seek God's guidance and then stay focused to that mission (Nehemiah 6:3).

52. Great leaders know how to wait out the opposition so that the real motive is revealed (Nehemiah 6:4-9).

53. Great leaders respond clearly and distinctly to slanderous situations. (Nehemiah 6:8-9).

54. Great leaders are willing and able to stand alone to share God's Word. (Nehemiah 8:3).

55. Great leaders know how to share their knowledge in such a manner that people understand (Nehemiah 8:7-8).

56. Great leaders conduct business in a manner that honors God and not the world (Nehemiah 10:31).

57. Great leaders use God's methods to motivate people (Nehemiah 11:2).

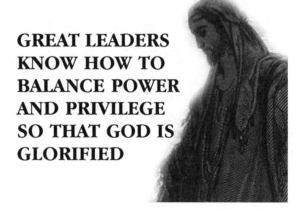

GREAT LEADERS KNOW HOW TO BALANCE POWER AND PRIVILEGE SO THAT GOD IS GLORIFIED

58. Great leaders know when to call on the experts in a particular field (Nehemiah 12:27).

59. Great leaders understand the problem before they take action (Nehemiah 13:1-7).

60. Great leaders do not allow evil to knowingly exist in their operations (Nehemiah 13:1-7).

61. Great leaders look for the problems in order to solve them (Nehemiah 13:10-14).

62. Great leaders know when they have to step in and clean house (Nehemiah 13:15-22). ■

THE WISDOM OF THE GEESE

All Scriptures are New King James Version unless otherwise indicated.

by Robin McMillan

The distinctive honking and V-shaped flight pattern of geese have intrigued mankind from the earliest time. Their migratory activity heralds the changing seasons. Nature is one of God's best classrooms. His creation reveals Him in our everyday experience, just as the Psalmist has written, **"The heavens declare the glory of God…" (Psalm 19:1).** Consider then, the wisdom of the geese. Much can be learned from them that applies to us in ministry.

THE WISDOM OF THEIR METHODS

Rick Joyner has often regarded the migratory flight methods of geese as containing valuable insights for people working together in teams. By traveling in the characteristic V-formation, the flapping of the wings creates uplift for each following fowl. Flying in the vortex created by the wingtip of each goose reduces wind resistance and conserves 50 percent of their energy, thus increasing their travel distance by 71 percent. These methods enable them to accomplish more corporately than they could individually. Modern stock car drivers have used similar drafting techniques to win races. We, too, must flow in harmony with others of like mind and common calling to maximize the gain from our efforts.

Just as geese enable each other to fly faster with less effort, we too may gain spiritually from this principle of corporate momentum. I have noticed that dramatic and rapid progress is made by less skillful people as they associate in ministry with others who function at a higher level. Flowing together in common ministry releases an impartation that is difficult to obtain while functioning alone.

THE LEAD GOOSE PRINCIPLE

The goose who leads the flight pattern expends the most energy because he encounters the most direct wind resistance. One characteristic of geese in flight is that when the lead goose tires, he drops out of his front position and falls back in the formation. We have recognized that there are times when the person leading a certain area of ministry needs a rest and someone else must assume the leadership. We must be sensitive to the energy levels of those around us, both for their good and the good of the team. If they remain in a depleted state they suffer unnecessarily and the momentum of the team is reduced. Moving out of the lead, yet continuing to function on the team, allows the individual an opportunity to become strengthened and lead again in the future.

GEESE HAVE ENDURANCE

The endurance of the geese should both challenge and encourage each of us. By drafting and changing leaders some species of geese fly over one thousand miles without resting. Imagine flapping and honking for more than a thousand miles, non-stop. Such endurance is the

direct result of flying in formation, using corporate momentum, and sharing the burden by laboring together. As we function together, God will reveal to us ways to work together to accomplish things that we once thought impossible and without exhausting anyone on our team.

> **Moving out of the lead, yet continuing to function on the team, allows the individual an opportunity to become strengthened and lead again in the future.**

GEESE ARE SENSITIVE

To perform at the maximum level, geese must be sensitive to wind resistance. When one slips out of place in the flight pattern, he immediately feels this resistance known as drag. Drag causes each goose to expend excess energy and affects the overall productivity of the group. Sensitivity enables the geese to make moment-by-moment adjustments and abide in their proper places. We must have the same sensitivity in recognizing the resistance we meet when we are not in our proper place. Jesus understood the importance of alignment. He said,

"Come to Me, all you who labor and are heavy laden, and I will give you rest.

Take My yoke upon you and learn from Me, for I am gentle and lowly in heart, and you will find rest for your souls.

For My yoke is easy and My burden is light" (Matthew 11:28-30).

> When we take Jesus' yoke and follow Him, He does most of the pulling. His yoke is easy as long as we pull in His direction.

Being yoked to Him is the key to empowered service. When two animals are yoked together, plowing is easier when they pull in the same direction. But if one of them pulls the wrong way, then they experience drag similar to geese who are out of sync in their formation. When we take Jesus' yoke and follow Him, He does most of the pulling. His yoke is easy as long as we pull in His direction. When our yoke gets inordinately hard, we should consider two things. Either we are out of alignment with Him and must make an adjustment, or we are yoked to something He has not given us.

GEESE ARE VERSATILE

Geese are incredibly versatile animals, being adept at functioning in three different environments. They are as at home on land and water as they are in the air. They have webbed feet, are good swimmers, and are equipped with bills which are suited to forage for food both on land and in the water.

The versatility of geese speaks of being well-rounded believers who function effectively in several different realms. Their proficiency in the air speaks of the believer's calling to a truly spiritual life. Geese fly at heights of up to one mile with the wind, sometimes being thrust forward by the currents of the jet stream. Wind is a type of the Holy Spirit, and as believers we should be adept at moving in the wind of His power. We should be as comfortable in the realm of supernatural gifts of the Spirit as we are in natural things. Signs and wonders should be as much a part of our normal lives as paying bills, loving and disciplining our children, or playing a round of golf.

GEESE ARE ENCOURAGERS

Geese honk at each other as they fly. It is their basic form of communication, helps them stay together, and encourages the leaders to keep up the pace. Believers should also be encouraging. It is one of the simplest ways we may serve one another. Everyone needs to be encouraged at one time or another. There are many negative and critical people who have done so much to harm the work of God. We should never be named among them. If you are going to honk, honk encouragingly, or keep your honking to yourself.

GEESE ARE LOYAL

Geese are loyal to their mates. Unlike other members of the animal kingdom, geese mate for life or until death. They are distinctly family oriented, often living with other related geese in extended families. They form such strong relationships that entire family units will often migrate together year after year.

Geese are extremely protective of their young. Mature geese are strong enough to ward off attacks of animals as large as foxes or coyotes. Some have observed male geese stopping traffic by standing upright and spreading their wings across the road, like a crossing guard guiding their young to safety. One driver noted that while a goose was standing in that position, he looked her right in the eyes until he knew she was not going to continue moving forward. Then he turned and helped his young cross the road to safety.

Geese protect their weak and wounded. It is well known that when a goose is sick and leaves the formation, another goose will follow it to the earth and remain with it until it recovers or dies. Later they will join another flight formation and instinctively make their way to their regular nesting ground.

In an article entitled "Honking Our Way Forward," Beth Miller relates the following: "Browne Barr tells a story about two geese who suddenly showed up on a small beach outside Tiburon, California, just north of San Francisco. The geese won the hearts of everyone when they discovered that one goose was blind and the other, the gander, had bravely sacrificed his migratory freedom to stay behind and keep his mate company."

Of all distinctive groups on the face of the earth, the church should embody faithfulness in marriage and loyalty among its members. In parts of the body of Christ, weak or wounded believers are often rejected and left behind. Although it is often difficult and challenging, we are to be as redemptive as people will allow us to be. I know personally that in some cases fallen or wounded believers are unwilling or unprepared to receive help. But when possible, we should do what is within our power to help restore every one of God's fallen children.

> It is well known that when a goose is sick and leaves the formation, another goose will follow it to the earth and remain with it until it recovers or dies.

The apostle Paul encouraged us to do just that; **"Brethren, if a man is overtaken in any trespass, you who are spiritual restore such a one in a spirit of gentleness, considering yourself lest you also be tempted" (Galatians 6:1).** How could we be redeemed by the mercy of God and yet have no heart for others who are in need? Paul expected no less from those who were truly spiritual. The very process of restoring those overtaken in a trespass can also safeguard us from temptation as we consider ourselves also. When we realize how easy it is to be trapped in any trespass, then we will with gentleness help those who are. Thus by realizing the deceitfulness of sin, and recognizing our own vulnerability, we will avoid much temptation.

> **Being renewed is a process of having constant encounters with the Lord where we exchange our strength for His.**

GEESE MOLT

From late June to late July geese molt and are grounded. During this time of renewal they exchange their old plumage for new flight feathers. So, also, must we experience a similar renewal. Isaiah prophesied: **"But those who wait on the LORD shall renew their strength; they shall mount up with wings like eagles, they shall run and not be weary, they shall walk and not faint"** (Isaiah 40:31). Being renewed is a process of having constant encounters with the Lord where we exchange our strength for His. If we do not take time to be restored and refreshed with Him, we will fall prey to our enemies. We become prey when we do not pray.

Not only should we have consistent time with Him, but we must also have regular times of rest and recreation. Thoroughly understanding human nature, the Lord instituted a regular weekly rest called the Sabbath. He knew many would work right on. One common trap among highly motivated Christians is that they are too busy to take vacations. True recreation is "re-creation," times to be created again, prepared for the next season of challenges.

GEESE HERALD A NEW SEASON

Geese are migratory by nature. This instinct enables them to discern the times and seasons for migration. Their survival depends on it. This migratory instinct compares to the spiritual gift of discernment and wisdom in issues of timing. Among King David's loyal soldiers were the sons of Issachar who were described this way: **"of the sons of Issachar who had understanding of the times, to know what Israel ought to do, their chiefs were two hundred; and all their brethren were at their command"** (I Chronicles 12:32). The sons of Issachar were prophetic men whose discernment was invaluable to the life of the nation. We also must learn to recognize those among us who have this sensitivity and listen to their counsel.

PICTURE OF FAITH AND HUMILITY

A goose is covered by several layers of feathers which protect it from the elements and enable it to fly. The longest and stiffest ones are the strong flight feathers located on their tail and wings. Underneath them is a thick layer of feathers called down, which is coated with natural oil and keeps water out and warmth in.

Both layers of feathers speak to us of vital spiritual truths. The strong outer feathers speak of the faith and courage we need to continually move forward. Paul himself encouraged us to continually arm ourselves with faith in order to conquer our adversaries, **"above all, taking the shield of faith with which you will be able to quench all the fiery darts of the wicked one" (Ephesians 6:16).**

The second layer of feathers, called down, bears its own unique message. Down is also a directional word that speaks of humility. We are exhorted to humble ourselves *"under* **the mighty hand of God" (I Peter 5:6).** Every high thing that has exalted itself against God is to be cast *down* (see II Corinthians 10:4-5). We bow *down* when we worship the Lord. When Jesus submitted himself to His parents at twelve years of age it was written of Him that He went *down*: **"Then He went *down* with them and came to Nazareth, and was subject to them, but His mother kept all these things in her heart" (Luke 2:51).** (Note: His going down and His coming to Nazareth were two different things. The phrase **"went down"** speaks of a spiritual attitude of heart submission and the phrase **"came to Nazareth"** was purely geographical).

One of the most important principles of the kingdom is contained in this short expression: **"God resists the proud, but gives grace to the humble" (I Peter 5:5).** Like geese we must all must have a protective layer of "down" to stay safe and abide in the grace of God. Humility is an essential quality for each of us.

> We must realize that in God the seasons are always new and He is always ready to enable His people to do great things.

IN CLOSING

I have received tremendous, personal encouragement over the years as I have heard the honking of the geese and watched them fly majestically through the southern skies. Each time I encounter them something stirs inside me of fresh hope and seasons of new possibilities. As I have written of these marvelous birds, that very sense has stirred in me again. We must realize that in God the seasons are always new and He is always ready to enable His people to do great things. It is time to arise. God is prepared to help us move ahead.

ACKNOWLEDGMENTS:

I have benefited from articles by Dr. Robert McNeish and Sue Widemark, who have written on the lessons found in the enlightening characteristics of geese. ■

THE TEST
OF PROPHETIC SERVANTS

All Scriptures are New King James Version.

by John Paul Jackson

Charles Dickens might have entitled his famous story "A Tale of Two Servants." They were two men, both with the opportunity to serve the most dynamic prophet of their generation. More than just simple servants, they were young prophets-in-training, being honed and sharpened by the best. And yet their paths were vastly different: one stayed with the seer until the very end, while the other left as soon as the going got rough. One fulfilled his prophetic destiny, and the other squandered it. They each had the same fiery test of loyalty and courage, but only one passed it.

Elijah's Two Servants

In I Kings 19, we read of the prophet Elijah's two servants. His first servant, who Scripture does not name, squandered his call. The evil Queen Jezebel was furious with Elijah and had ordered that he be killed. Life under a death sentence held no appeal for Elijah's servant. Scripture tells us what happened: **"and** [Elijah] **left his servant there" (I Kings 19:3).** Elijah fled into the wilderness, alone, and his servant did not bother going with him.

Why do you suppose this servant stayed in Beersheba? Remember, Elijah was a hunted man. So, perhaps he was afraid of dying. But whatever the servant's excuse, his lack of courage and endurance robbed him of the honor of walking with Elijah through some of the most magnificent moments God and man have ever shared. He was not fed by angels as Elijah was. He did not hear God's still, small voice on the mountain. This servant's inability to take risks cost him his future destiny.

God tells Elijah to anoint a new servant, Elisha (see verse 16). Even with the death sentence still looming large over the prophet, Elisha did not hesitate to say "yes" to the invitation of serving Elijah. He bid farewell to his family and set out for his future. Little did he know that it would take years of humble service before he would walk into the ultimate purpose for his life.

Elijah and Elisha ended up having spent many years together in ministry. During that time, Elisha faced the same test as Elijah's former servant. Three times, Elisha was asked by Elijah to stay at various places—Gilgal, Bethel, and Jericho—and three times he refused to leave the prophet's side. Elisha was different than the other servant; he recognized the tests facing him and determined to not squander his calling.

Even when the chariot of God swooped down from heaven and flew between Elisha and Elijah, the faithful servant never took his eyes off his mentor (see II Kings 2). Now let's pause a moment. Imagine what this chariot of God looked like—it must have been stunningly beautiful. Talk about a glorious distraction. Wow! We might be tempted to gaze upon such a glorious sight. Yet even the gold and glory of the heavenly realm did not mean as much to Elisha as his godly covenant to his friend. He kept his eyes fixed on

MANY OF US, LIKE THESE FOUR PROPHETIC SERVANTS, ARE GOING THROUGH TESTS THAT ARE MORE IMPORTANT THAN WE REALIZE.

his master and passed this final test. As a result, Elisha walked into his future, having inherited twice the anointing Elijah had.

Elijah's two servants had taken opposing paths. The first servant lost everything. The second servant, Elisha, stepped into his destiny, fulfilling that which God had created him to do.

Elisha's Two Servants

Later in Scripture it is recorded that Elisha's own servants faced a similar test. His first protégé, Gehazi, disobeyed him (see II Kings 5) and tried to swap God's blessing for financial gain. As a result, Gehazi and his descendants were cursed with leprosy. Gehazi had failed his test.

Elisha's second servant, however, did not abandon the prophet's side—even as a great army surrounded the two, threatening to kill them both (see II Kings 6). Because of his obedience and steadfastness, this second servant's eyes were opened to "see" into the coexisting spiritual realm at levels we have never even imagined. A significant test had been passed.

Many of us, like these four prophetic servants, are going through tests that are more important than we realize. The Apostle Peter called these tests "fiery trials," and beseeched us to stand fast in the face of them.

"Beloved, do not think it strange concerning the fiery trial which is to try you, as though some strange thing happened to you;

but rejoice to the extent that you partake of Christ's sufferings, that when His glory is revealed, you may also be glad with exceeding joy" (I Peter 4:12-13).

We are called to stand firm and relish God's testing. In the book of Hebrews, we are instructed to run the race of faith:

"Therefore we also, since we are surrounded by so great a cloud of witnesses, let us lay aside every weight, and the sin which so easily ensnares us, and let us run with endurance the race that is set before us,

looking unto Jesus, the author and finisher of our faith, who for the joy that was set before Him endured the cross, despising the shame, and has sat down at the right hand of the throne of God" (Hebrews 12:1-2).

Promotion is Coming

A season of divine promotion is upon us. The Lord is raising up people through the spiritual ranks, giving them an opportunity to serve Him at a higher level than ever before. Such promotion requires

testing, for God wants to ensure that His children can handle the responsibilities He intends to give them.

We will pass these fiery trials by running the race faithfully. We must not accept undue honor, glory, gold, or prestige. Instead we must remain humble in heart and try not to promote ourselves to others. If we take the risks God has for us, keeping our eyes completely on Him, He will promote us and we will finish the race well. Our eyes can be opened to "see" into the spiritual realm at levels of which we have never dreamed.

THE LORD IS RAISING UP PEOPLE THROUGH THE SPIRITUAL RANKS, GIVING THEM AN OPPORTUNITY TO SERVE HIM AT A HIGHER LEVEL THAN EVER BEFORE.

This spring, many of you will "pass the test" and see a marked increase in the fruit in your life. Please take time every day to pray and ask the Lord to reveal to you those issues that might disqualify you from walking into the fullness of your divine purpose.

I cannot stress the importance of doing this and the subsequent impact upon your destiny. You might say this is a time of visitation. There will be many levels of divine visitation, depending on where you are in your spiritual walk. If you pass the tests before you, each new season will promise an even deeper level than the previous one.

We need only to keep our eyes focused fully on the Master, humbly submitting to all He requires of us. What lies ahead will be worth it all! ∎

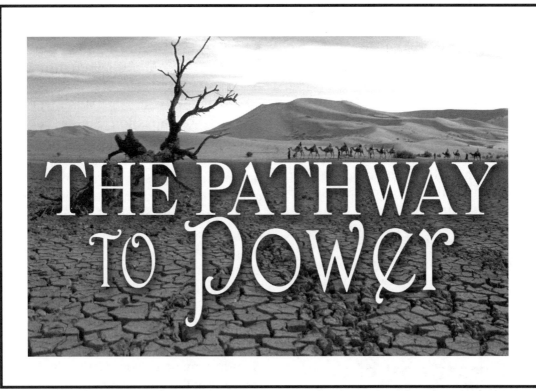

THE PATHWAY TO Power

by Francis Frangipane

A new awakening is coming to the church. It will be birthed by prayer and sheltered by humility, but its power will emerge through compassion. The strength of this fresh move is the deep yearning of the Lord Himself. Yes, even in the midst of hellish conditions on earth, He has promised, **"I will have mercy on whom I will have mercy, and I will have compassion on whom I have compassion" (Romans 9:15).**

Common people, flooded and compelled by the burning compassion of God, shall be used mightily in the coming years—they shall transform multitudes. Christ's compassion shall especially be revealed where human suffering is unrelenting. Let us remember, the Lord is not aloof from the human condition; mankind's suffering exists in the thought-life of God. The book of Judges reveals an amazing quality about the relationship of God's heart to human sorrow. Scripture says, **"He could bear the misery of Israel no longer" (Judges 10:16).** As a result, He rescued His people from their enemies.

Today, the Holy Spirit says, "The more devastated the region, the greater My compassion shall flow." Africa and parts of Asia shall see multitudes convert from Islam and come into a powerful relationship with Christ. Indeed, during Ramadan, the Islamic holy month, many Muslims shall have visions of Jesus Christ and shall be converted, as Paul was converted from Judaism.

Missionaries from Pakistan shall be used by God to touch many nations. The Holy Spirit says, "Pray fervently for Pakistan, for its President, General Pervez Musharraf, and for the church in Pakistan, for missionaries from Pakistan shall reveal Christ's compassion to many nations." Additionally, the Lord says, "Pray for and watch India." India's hour is drawing near. Satan would like to destroy these two countries before the great outpouring of the Holy Spirit falls upon them. Thus, the Holy Spirit commands, "Pray for Pakistan and India!"

Yet, this move of divine compassion will not be limited to poorer nations. In select cities and communities in the West, the compassion of God will also flow. Indeed, even now the Lord is preparing Christians from all backgrounds, including believing Catholics, Presbyterians, and Episcopalians. Some whom God will use most mightily will come from denominations many Christians consider dead or apostate.

> Because most of us have been exhausted by the limits of our compassion, we must submit again to the opening of our hearts.

Many influential, but hardened businessmen and women will be touched and transformed by the compassion of God. Governors, mayors, and other civic leaders will experience life-changing healings; attorneys, doctors, and scientists will testify to undeniable miracles. Transformed gang leaders and criminals, some of whom are currently in jail, will be used by God to start powerful churches. Yes, once seemingly hopeless criminals will be used by God to bring hope to devastated neighborhoods.

The Key to Power: Divine Compassion

Because the taproot of this revival will be compassion, it is important to isolate it from other virtues and inspired ministry gifts. For one can be a skilled teacher who functions authentically in communication skills, but not have true compassion. A leader might possess effective administrative skills, yet also be void of compassion. Simply because one is a gifted psalmist and leads many in Christian music and arts, this does not mean he or she is empowered by compassion in their ministry. Yes, even the most stirring of the prophets or apostles may himself be stirred by something other than compassion. All of these gifts and ministries can be truly inspired within the parameters of their functionality, but not carry at their core the deep pulse of God's compassion.

The word most often translated in the New Testament as "compassion" means "a yearning in the bowels." It is not a function of the intellect, but a deeper reality of the spirit. Thus, it is important we do not let religious intellectualism rule us. True compassion emerges from the compassion of God; the human channel of His compassion must be united with the yearnings of God. Because most of us have been exhausted by the limits of our compassion, we must submit again to the opening of our hearts. Trust God to help, for we must learn to surrender afresh to the fire of compassion's quest.

Consider also beloved, that this "yearning in the bowels," this "innermost being," is the very region from which Jesus said **"rivers of living water" (John 7:38)** shall flow. This new level of compassion will not exhaust with mere impotent sympathy, but will instead align our spirits with the power of Christ to heal, save, and redeem.

Compassion is stronger than sympathy and more enduring than empathy—both of which are dimensions of vulnerability and identification—through essential escorts that lead us to Christ's compassion. Compassion, however, captures those feelings and transforms them into love-empowered actions.

Consider Christ as He healed the afflicted in the gospels: **"moved with compassion, He stretched out His hand and touched him, and said to him, 'I am willing [to heal you]; be cleansed' "** (Mark 1:41). Again we read, **"moved with compassion, Jesus touched their eyes; and immediately they regained their sight and followed Him (Matthew 20:34).** And again, **"when He went ashore, He saw a great multitude, and felt compassion for them, and healed their sick" (Matthew 14:14).**

Jesus was moved with compassion; He felt it, and He **"healed their sick."** Do we feel compassion? Are we aware today of compassion's inner pushing? Can you list when you too were **"moved with compassion?"** Too often, instead of compassion, we are moved by ambition, self-interest, and pride. We desire to be seen by men, to be admired for the size and scope of our ministries or talents. In our zeal to fulfill our passion, we miss compassion. May God deliver us! To many, the multitudes are symbols of power and success. Yet, when Jesus saw the crowds, He did not see them as a means to personal fulfillment. Rather, **"...He felt compassion for them, because they were distressed and downcast like sheep without a shepherd" (Matthew 9:36).**

The people had Pharisees, but not shepherds; they endured the influence of doctrinal experts, the "lawyers," but they had no one who truly cared for them. Christ felt compassion, was moved by compassion, and let compassion find its fulfillment in the healing and comfort of the sick and afflicted.

I am not speaking of others, beloved. We ourselves have locked our compassion and restrained the yearnings of God within us. In this day it is not enough for us merely to be friendly or nice; we must allow the Spirit to unlock the bowels of our compassion. The Lord has promised, not only will He have mercy on many and lead them into forgiveness and salvation, but that He will also reveal His great compassion. Let me repeat His promised, irrevocable purpose: **"I will have compassion on whom I have compassion"** (Romans 9:15).

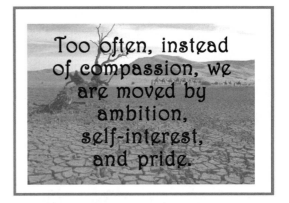

The Lord is with us to fulfill His great yearning to save and heal. He has set His heart to reveal His compassion in this hour; we must allow His compassion to move us. We have learned how to have church, to produce Sunday morning events which stir and excite. Now, however, the Lord says, **"But go and learn what this means: 'I DESIRE COMPASSION, AND NOT SACRIFICE'" (Matthew 9:13).** He tells us to not look beyond the hardened or the hopeless. He reminds us, **"for I did not come to call the righteous, but sinners" (Matthew 9:13).** Compassion is the pathway to power. ■

The COMING OF THE KINGDOM

by Rick Joyner

In Luke 17:20-21, the Lord gives us an important insight as to how we will discern the coming of His kingdom:

> **Now having been questioned by the Pharisees as to when the kingdom of God was coming, He answered them and said, "The kingdom of God is not coming with signs to be observed;**
>
> **nor will they say, "Look, here it is!' or, "There it is!' For behold, the kingdom of God is in your midst."**

In this discourse, the Lord basically tells us that if we are overly focused on outward signs, we will not perceive the coming of His kingdom. It is going to come in a way more subtle than most are going to be looking for. It will even be "in our midst" while most are completely unaware of it.

Even though we know the kingdom will not fully come until the King Himself returns, we are here to prepare the way for His coming. We do this by preaching the coming of His kingdom, and by laying a foundation for that kingdom.

Even though it is has been argued for generations that the mission of preaching His kingdom has not yet been accomplished, but only the gospel of salvation has gone forth, before the end comes we will know that the gospel of the kingdom has been preached throughout the world. It is apparent this is still a future event that is yet to be finished.

Though we should rejoice in the preaching of the gospel of salvation, and the spreading of the good news of all that Jesus accomplished for us at the cross, the gospel of the kingdom is not just about the salvation of man, it is about the lordship of Christ Jesus.

I have heard quite a few say that they came to know Jesus as Savior at a certain point in their life, and then came to know Him as Lord at a later time. This is good, but His lordship over us as individuals should be fully revealed at the time of salvation. Even so, the gospel of the kingdom is more than Jesus being revealed as Lord over us as individuals—it is the proclamation of Jesus as Lord over all, both in the heavens and on the earth. This is yet to be done, and is actually the last trumpet, or message, that will go forth, as is written in the book of Revelation.

It is when we see this gospel being preached in all the world that we will know the end of this age is near, and the coming of His kingdom is truly at hand. Even though this is yet to be done, preparation for it is now going on, and there are many other ways in which the foundation for the kingdom is being laid in the earth. This is not being done in such a way that great, outward signs can be observed. We must have "eyes to see" in order to behold it and to be a part of preparing the world for His kingdom.

The Paradox

As a student of history and revivals, I have often wondered why many church historians view changing society as evidence that a move of God was truly from God. I can understand it in the light of this being evidence of the church becoming the light and salt to the world that it is supposed to be. But I have been concerned because many movements have lost their focus and energy by prematurely trying to reform society when the church had not yet been truly renewed and restored. The end result of this has usually been that little was accomplished for either.

It is also interesting to me that the prophetic leaders, who accomplished the most in reforming society, often had little or no vision for doing this. They were simply serving the gospel and seeking to help revive the household of faith. It was in this way that the first century apostles impacted the world more than any conqueror in history even though they did not seem to be trying. The light in them was too powerful for the darkness and the great substance of their character could not help but to impact the world in their time.

> It is when we see this gospel being preached in all the world that we will know the end of this age is near, and the coming of His kingdom is truly at hand.

The Power of Life Within

Another great saint in church history who had just such an impact was Jon Amos Comenius. Like the apostles, the impact of his life continues to shape the world many generations after him. Though he lived four hundred years ago, he not only was one of the handful of men most responsible for shaping the modern world, he is one of a handful who have had a major influence in laying the foundation for the coming of the kingdom.

Comenius was a Moravian bishop who lived in the early 1600s. He was a pastor within a small group of believers called "Hussites." They were called this because they held to the teachings of John Huss, the great Czech reformer and martyr, who prophesied the Reformation nearly one hundred years before Martin Luther, which many consider to be the birth of the Reformation. When Huss was being burned at the stake for refusing to compromise his convictions of the truth, he prophesied that the seed which would reform the church would fall into the ground and die, but in due time it would sprout and bear fruit. Huss knew that this would happen because he understood the power of the life in him. Men could kill his body but they could not kill the life that comes from God. That life had to rise again.

> To prepare the church for this, Comenius perceived and preached that the church had to take up its mandate for education.

Comenius lived over one hundred years after Luther, and two hundred years after Huss. Even though the movement that Luther helped to spark was considered the beginning of the Reformation (the reformation of the church), Comenius maintained that the seed Huss had spoken about had not yet sprouted, but would one hundred years after his own time. Comenius believed this seed that Huss planted would result in the Great Commission being fulfilled. Though the Reformation had begun with the revelation of personal salvation and responsibility, rather than being saved by being a part of an institution, it seemed to quickly become sidetracked into a political movement, and then began to fracture as politics do.

Even though Comenius was caught in the crossfire of political/religious wars all of his life, he was able to stay above the fray. He remained relentlessly focused on preparing the church for the time in which it would rise up to fulfill the Great Commission.

To prepare the church for this, Comenius perceived and preached that the church had to take up its mandate for education. He said the church was called to be the light of the world, and light was illumination, which was education. In this way he became the first, and possibly the only, true genius to work in the field of education. For this reason he is called "the father of modern education." His influence is so expansive that many not only count him among the handful who have had the greatest impact on the modern world, but also for the spark that ignited the torch of knowledge, the flames of which have accelerated in the world since his time.

Fulfilling the Great Commission

Even though Comenius was hired by governments to start systems of public education, to which he did devote some time, his vision for education was to prepare the church to fulfill the Great Commission. He believed that education was the special mandate of the church because the Great Commission was not to just make converts, but to **"make disciples,"** which are students, teaching them to observe all that Jesus commanded. He also maintained that the Great Commission was to make disciples of **"all nations,"** not just individuals (see Matthew 28:19).

The reason Comenius helped the governments to start public education was because they were considered "Christian governments," with godly kings who wanted their people given a Christian education. Comenius saw such Christian governments as being the foundation of the kingdom of God which was to come. This was also the basic theology of many of the colonists settling in America at the time, who were devoted to raising up a Christian nation. It was because of this that Comenius was asked to be the first president of Harvard University, which he turned down only because of his work in Europe.

It was almost one hundred years after Comenius had prophesied that the seed Huss had spoken about would sprout when the young Count Zinzendorf happened upon Comenius' writings in the library of Dresden, Germany. These gave him the vision for modern missions, thus seeming to dramatically fulfill Comenius' prophecy that the seed would sprout one hundred years after his time. However, what few have put together is that the seedbed in which this seed sprouted was education. It was actually the same spiritual seed which gave birth to both modern missions and modern education. The two go together and are inseparable in preparing for the Great Commission to be fulfilled, and for laying a foundation for the kingdom to come.

It is because modern education has become mostly secularized that much of the life force needed for fulfilling the Great Commission has been robbed by the deceiver. This must be recovered. Missions and education go together. Separating the two has caused a tragic reduction of both. This is the special mandate of the church which will fulfill the Great Commission—combine missions with education.

As Comenius taught, we cannot be the light of the world without being devoted to true education. We cannot fulfill the Great Commission without being devoted to true education. Making disciples who learn to observe "all that He has commanded" requires far more than an hour in Sunday school each week. The true Christian life is not something that we give a few hours to each week, but true Christianity is a life so devoted to Christ that it is the center and motive for all we do.

> It is because modern education has become mostly secularized that much of the life force needed for fulfilling the Great Commission has been robbed by the deceiver.

I also am using the term "true education," meaning education devoted to truth. As Comenius proclaimed, because all things were made for Christ and through Him, all true education will lead to Him. He called nature "God's second book," understanding what Paul wrote in Romans chapter one that the Lord's ways are clearly seen through the things that are made. The study of all things that are made should lead to Him. All true science will lead to the Creator. All true knowledge will lead to a greater understanding of the ways of the Lord.

The reason there is such a perversion in the pursuit of knowledge today is because the church has surrendered her mandate for education, and as with all authority which man surrenders, Satan picked it up to use it for evil. Even so, this mandate will be retaken by the church. This is even being done at this time in a way which will soon begin to have a great impact on the entire world—preparation for the coming kingdom.

> While proclaiming it is teaching liberty and reason, public education has also become one of the most powerful forces binding and discouraging creativity.

A Renewed Church Will Renew Minds

As we are told in Romans 12:2, **"And do not be conformed to this world, but be transformed by the renewing of your mind, that you may prove what the will of God is, that which is good and acceptable and perfect."** To be able to **"prove what the will of God is"** we must have renewed minds. How can we turn our children over to the world five days a week to have their minds formed and expect them to have renewed minds? This is why many of them walk in more confusion than clarity about the will of God in their life.

There are many movements today that are called "renewal movements." They have brought great blessing to the advancing church throughout the world. It is also apparent that each one of these was intended to help bring about a renewing of the minds of those who are pursuing God. One basic characteristic of the true church, and a true Christian, is that they do not think the same way the world thinks. However, to have a "renewed" mind also implies having a *newness*. There is a freshness and power of creativity which is the hallmark of a truly renewed mind. We do not want to just think differently, we want to think "new."

The Slaughterhouse of the Mind

Not only is modern, public education becoming more and more anti-Christ in its teachings, it is also being filled with more and more sexual, moral, and ethical perversion. Public education has become the number one force corrupting the souls of our children. Sin, and even witchcraft, can be openly taught in public schools in America, while just the mention of Christ can bring expulsion. One has to be blind not to understand that public schools in general have now become a stronghold of the anti-Christ spirit.

While proclaiming it is teaching liberty and reason, public education has also become one of the most powerful forces binding and discouraging creativity. With but few exceptions, the system of education rewards mediocrity and penalizes creativity and initiative. Claiming to be setting children free from ancient and archaic moral standards, they impose the greatest bondage of all, bondage of the minds enforced by their ruthless thought police. This is a primary way in which Satan blinds the minds and keeps mankind in subjection to him to do his will. The actual "freedom" that most public education promotes is the freedom to sin and be accepted while being perverted.

Comenius taught that knowledge is glorious, and that schools should be a piece of heaven. Instead, schools in our time have become a piece of hell, and as Comenius himself once lamented, they have now become "slaughterhouses of the mind."

The church is called to be **"the light of the world," (Matthew 5:14)** and light is illumination, or education. That is why the Great Commission is not only about making converts, but also making them lifelong students of the Lord who are ever passionate about learning His ways. The church must again take up this mandate for education, making true knowledge glorious, because true knowledge will always reveal the glory of our great Creator.

Even so, presently "Christian schools," for the most part are little better than secular schools. It is good that they teach the creation, and other biblical principles, but because most have adopted the basic system of education used in public schools, many Christian schools are just as prone to punish creativity and initiative.

One basic principle of true education is that all who are coming to know the Creator are going to become creative. In fact, a basic aspect of the One who so loves creativity and diversity is that He even makes every snowflake different. If we are going to be like Him, we will be creative. No one should be more creative than those who are coming to know their Creator. Christian education also needs to be "born again" in many ways, so it releases true creativity. There is a power in creativity that will shape the world, and it will be prophetic creativity which helps prepare the way for the coming King—who is the Creator.

The Place of Public Education

Even though I believe I have stated sober truth about the general state of public education, I do not mean to imply that everything is wrong in public education, or Christian education. Public education would not be in near the state it is in today if it had not been seized by liberal, secular humanists, and others with a perverted agenda, such as the homosexual community. These are using education to change society to the way they think it should be. They have long-term goals, and they have implemented them very effectively, even to the point of removing all mention of God from the classroom, and now public life in general. This was done mostly because Christians did nothing, but continually allowed the enemy to tear off large pieces of our spiritual territory with little or no fight.

> There is a power in creativity that will shape the world, and it will be prophetic creativity which helps prepare the way for the coming King—who is the Creator.

Even so, public education has a place, and we should have some influence in it if the church is going to be the salt and light of the world. Because a plane is hijacked does not mean the plane is evil. Blowing up such a plane should only be a last resort. Let us try to retake control of the plane first.

The Power of Freedom

Now, two of our most basic freedoms, and linchpins of all true freedom, the freedom of speech and the freedom of religion, are in jeopardy in almost every nation that claims to be a part of "the free world." Now, just as I prophesied in 1988 in my book, *The Harvest,* the nations which were at that time under the heaviest yoke of bondage, communism, have greater freedom of religion and speech than in Europe or America. Europe and America are heading toward greater repression, and the former communist countries are moving toward increasing liberty.

> **Christians, in general, need their own schools, built upon the only foundation that will remain, and that will survive the shaking that is coming upon the world.**

Of course there are strong forces of repression still in power in the former communist countries, which do arise from time to time to try to thwart or delay the advance of liberty, but they will not succeed. However, in the countries that have enjoyed liberty for so long, such as the United States, the reverse is happening. Repression is relentlessly advancing and it is only occasionally that those committed to liberty rise up to fight this encroaching repression.

Even though this has become true, we must not give up on Europe or America yet. There is great hope that change is coming. Both are close to experiencing a great spiritual awakening which could very well reverse overnight the most carefully laid plans of the enemy to further corrupt and bind the nations. However, to win this battle we must fight on the most strategic battlefield of all—education.

Even so, religion imposed will never be true religion. You can make a parrot say and do the right things, but it will never be in his heart. Our goal should never be to just make people behave the way we want to them to, but our goal should be to help them want to obey in order to please the Lord. This can only come from a sincere love of God.

For this reason I am personally very thankful for public education. I think that all children should have the opportunity for a good education, with the freedom not to have to submit to any form of religious education, if that is their will.

There are also many fine public schools whose systems have resisted the tendency to actually become promoters of the religion of secular humanism. Some have also resisted the tendency of becoming blatantly anti-Christian in what they teach. Even so, these are becoming increasingly rare, and in many public schools new age doctrines and practices, as well as other religions, are openly taught. And as stated previously, many even allow witchcraft to be promoted and taught, while the very mention of Christ can result in expulsion. Very few public schools are truly neutral in their religious teaching, but there are some.

I do not believe that Christians should totally abandon public schools to the devil and the perversions which are gradually taking them over, but should stand boldly against these influences. Even so, our ultimate victory in education cannot be built upon the foundation of public education. The only foundation that will stand is the foundation of Jesus Christ. Christians, in general, need their own schools, built upon the only foundation that will remain and survive the shaking which is coming upon the world.

When Christians rise up, and take up their mandate for education, they will raise up schools with which no one else can compete. Then, even the heathen will beat a path to the door of the church to have their children educated. This is actually beginning to happen now in some places, which we will discuss more momentarily. However, I want to drive home a little more the essential element of creativity in school, as well as church life.

True Worship Requires True Liberty

First, there can be no true religion without liberty. There will be no true worship from the heart unless there is the freedom not to worship. This is why the Lord put the Tree of the Knowledge of Good and Evil in the Garden in the first place. There could be no true obedience from man if there was no freedom to disobey. Without this freedom the Lord would have been better off to have just created the computer instead of man, programming it to worship Him just the way He wanted. Of course, such worship is not worship at all, but a program in which our "living God" could never take pleasure.

For this reason the church needs to examine many of its "programs." Is it truly worship that touches the Lord when we command everyone to stand and sing songs which are basically the reading of words from a book? Are our other "programs" working true obedience from the heart?

I personally love hymns, and believe they do have a place in church life. Even the Lord Jesus sang hymns with His disciples. There are also programs that can accomplish much. It is the discipline of a program, the result of using knowledge which others have tried and found to work, which keeps us from having to continually "reinvent the wheel" in many things. However, if we are really going to touch the Lord with our worship, it must come from the heart of those serving Him, not just repeating what others have said, written, or done.

> My point is that there must be a release and promotion of creativity in the church, and in Christian schools, if we are going to have a faith, or a worship, which touches the Lord.

As a parent, it means something to me for my children to buy me a picture, especially when I know they have carefully selected one they think I will like. However, even though a picture they buy for me may look better, it will never touch me nearly as much as one they have drawn or painted themselves for me personally. My point is that there must be a release and promotion of creativity in the church, and in Christian schools, if we are going to have a faith, or a worship, which touches the Lord.

Have you ever wondered why some of the people are listed as the great heroes of faith in Hebrews 11? There really seems to be only one common denominator among all of these—they all did something that no one had ever done before. They were creative in their faith.

There is something about having faith to press beyond the limits of our times that touches God more than any other kind of faith. This is because it touches the very core of His being. The Creator is first and foremost, creative. Everything He does is touched by creativity. Have you ever wondered why Jesus seems never to heal in the same way twice? Even His healing was so creative that it was a very special, personal touch for each one He healed.

> They were not doing this just because of their higher academic standards, but because they wanted their children to have the strong moral and ethical foundations which were being imparted in these schools.

The Kingdom Is Coming in Education

For many years I have heard prophetic words about how a move of God was going to originate in Australia and New Zealand which would have a great impact at the end of this age, helping to prepare for the age to come. While recently in both of these countries I saw the seeds of these movements beginning to sprout. In some ways they are even more than sprouting, they have grown and are bearing fruit.

The night before I left on my trip to Australia and New Zealand, while I was playing a strategic board game with my two sons, the Lord spoke to me above the clamor of our game and told me that I was about to go to two of the most strategic nations on earth at this time. This really got my attention to be alert for signs of something of great significance being born there. I was not disappointed. Now let me tell you what I saw, and then explain what it foreshadows for the rest of the world.

The government in Australia is beginning to acknowledge that it cannot compete with private schools in providing quality education. Obviously caring more for their children than just keeping their dominion over education, this government is moving toward *the privatization of education.*

This is taking remarkable political courage and foresight, and great nobility of spirit, since it is certainly not without opposition—but in some ways they are also acknowledging what is inevitable.

In Australia, the forefront of private education is the Christian schools. When I was in Sydney I happened upon a newspaper article which indicated that one-third of all students in New South Wales (the state Sydney is in) are now in Christian schools. In this article, Muslims, atheists, and those of almost every other major religion, were putting their children in Christian schools, not just private schools. What surprised me was that they were not doing this just because of their higher academic standards, but because they wanted their children to have the strong moral and ethical foundations which were being imparted in these schools. They said simply that there was nowhere else this was being done.

When I discussed this with some from Queensland, another Australian state, they assured me that the same was true there as well. Others assured me that it was true of the whole country. My conclusion was that this is now such a strong movement, it is only a matter of time before all schools in Australia are privatized, basically getting the government out of the education business. It was obvious to all that the private schools could and were doing a much better job with education. They were so much better that the public schools just could not compete with them.

Hope for All

Few things would probably help governments more than having the burden of education removed from them. The main reason a government would even *want* to be involved in education is to impose its agenda and philosophy on its people, which any government devoted to liberty would not want to do. A valid reason would be to insure that all of its people have the opportunity of an education.

So how can we insure that all children have the opportunity of an education, without having a religion or philosophy imposed on them? Christians who are in pursuit of true obedience and worship of the Lord should want this. One answer is that industries and corporations should get in the education business. This would release a remarkable and refreshing diversity and competition in education which would carry education to increasingly more effective developments.

Would this not threaten Christian schools? Not at all. Because the Lord has given a special mandate for education to His church, and an **"anointing that teaches you about all things," (I John 2:27)** true Christian schools that are led by the Holy Spirit would excel even more in this environment.

It has been said for decades in America that the wheels are coming off of public education. I think they have certainly been wobbling, and in some places have come off, but in general the breakdown has not come completely, but soon will. There are success stories in public education, and some real heroes are making great things happen in nearly impossible situations.

These educators should be appreciated and honored. However, there are far more stories of defeats and tragedies than there are stories of victories. The world is going to be forced to move toward the privatization of education, in which Australia has become a courageous leader.

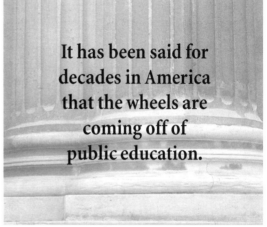

It has been said for decades in America that the wheels are coming off of public education.

Many teachers, and certainly teacher's unions, can be expected to be very threatened by this development, and to fight it. However, no one has more to gain from this than the teachers. Their value and esteem, in such a competitive system of privatized education, will almost certainly multiply.

Most governments of the world are now starting to face the fact that at the very least something is profoundly wrong with public education. Some are starting to say, even publicly, that maybe the government should not even be in the education business. This belief will grow into movements, and then we will eventually see the privatization of education begin to sweep the world.

It is crucial that the church foresee this great opportunity, which is coming, and be prepared for it. It is crucial to the fulfillment of the Great Commission, as well as preparing the way for the kingdom to come.

Discern the Kingdom

There is another factor which we also need to understand about the coming of the kingdom. We have come to the time that is described in Hebrews 12:25-29:

> Everything which has not been built on the only foundation that can stand, Jesus Christ, will be removed.

> See to it that you do not refuse Him who is speaking. For if those did not escape when they refused him who warned them on earth, much less shall we escape who turn away from Him who warns from heaven.

> And His voice shook the earth then, but now He has promised, saying, "YET ONCE MORE I WILL SHAKE NOT ONLY THE EARTH, BUT ALSO THE HEAVEN."

> This expression, "Yet once more," denotes the removing of those things which can be shaken, as of created things, so that those things which cannot be shaken may remain.

> Therefore, since we receive a kingdom which cannot be shaken, let us show gratitude, by which we may offer to God an acceptable service with reverence and awe;

> for our God is a consuming fire.

Everything which has not been built on the only foundation that can stand, Jesus Christ, will be removed. When these begin to shake, like education is now shaking, that which is built upon the Rock, Jesus, will emerge. This is the principle declared in Nebuchadnezzar's dream of the statue, which Daniel interpreted (see Daniel 2).

This statue represented the great empires of men that would have dominion over a great part of mankind. These were struck in the foot by a stone that grew into a mountain, and then filled the whole earth. This stone of course is Christ, and the mountain is His kingdom. Since the kingdoms of this world are now shaking and beginning to collapse, His kingdom is going to be growing.

Many also have a concept that when the Lord returns, the world will become instantly perfect. That is not how it will happen. Of course, with Satan bound and the Lord present on the earth, things will get much better instantly, but it will take the entire one thousand year period to fully restore the earth from its fallen condition. As Peter stated it in Acts 3:19-21:

> "Repent therefore and return, that your sins may be wiped away, in order that times of refreshing may come from the presence of the Lord;

and that He may send Jesus, the Christ appointed for you,

whom heaven must receive until the period of restoration of all things about which God spoke by the mouth of His holy prophets from ancient time."

Here he speaks of "**the period of restoration.**" This is the one thousand year reign of Christ on the earth. It will not happen all at once. Just like a wise relay runner gives the right attention to how the baton is passed if they want to win the race, the Lord is already preparing to take over the world. In many ways the passing of the batons of authority and influence are even now being passed to His people.

The Lord could have bound Satan and begun this period of restoration immediately after His resurrection. The entire church age has been for the calling forth, testing, and maturing of those who are called to rule and reign with Him over the earth. These will be resurrected to a heavenly nature and body like His, and will be given dominion over cities and regions of the earth. They will bring about its complete restoration to the state which God originally intended it to be. This is when we will see peace so restored to the earth that the lions will lie down with lambs, children will play with cobras, and no one will be hurt.

To fulfill the Great Commission is to begin to prepare the world for the coming kingdom. We should not presume that we can build anything now which will be as good as it will become in the kingdom age, but we are called to lay a

foundation for it now. This accomplishes two crucial things:

1) It will make the transition smoother, and
2) It lays a foundation in those who are called to rule and reign with Christ, a heart for and understanding of this restoration.

> We should not presume that we can build anything now which will be as good as it will become in the kingdom age, but we are called to lay a foundation for it now.

Contention Between Pre and Post Tribulation Rapture Doctrines

Though I have read articles on this issue (none of which have been accurate), I do not believe that holding to either of these views negates what I am sharing here, or the preparation which we are called to make for the coming kingdom of God. The most basic understanding of the Great Commission, or our calling to be the salt and light in this world, requires this devotion. I am not trying to use what I have addressed here to either promote one view about the timing of the rapture, or refute the other.

Even though it seems that most who hold to the pre-tribulation rapture theory develop an "escape mentality" that hinders their effectiveness as Christians, which is unfruitful, it does not by itself negate the doctrine. There are multitudes who became Christians after reading such books as, *The Late Great Planet Earth,* and the *Left Behind Series.* These have become incredibly powerful evangelistic tools, and how can we not rejoice in this and acknowledge it as good fruit?

> The people who really know their God never retreat before the enemies of the cross, but will always be found as people of action regardless of how inevitable defeat may seem, or how unlikely victory may seem.

That many assume, in contrast to the teaching of Scripture, that we should just get ready to abandon the earth because the devil is going to take it over, is unfortunate. Daniel 11: 31-32 tells us what attitude we should have even in the face of the anti-Christ:

> "And forces from him will arise, desecrate the sanctuary fortress, and do away with the regular sacrifice. And they will set up the abomination of desolation.
>
> "By smooth words he will turn to godlessness those who act wickedly toward the covenant, but the people who know their God will display strength and take action.

Even when the **"abomination of desolation"** is being set up, **"the people who know their God will display strength and take action."** The people who really know their God never retreat before the enemies of the cross, but will always be found as people of action regardless of how inevitable defeat may seem, or how unlikely victory may seem. They will be faithful, which means "full of faith," regardless of what circumstances they are found in. True faith knows that the more impossible the situation looks, the more God seems to enjoy it, and the more marvelous His sure victory will be.

For now we must be faithful to what is clearly revealed in the Scriptures, and treat with grace those who hold to different views of the more ambiguous biblical prophecies. One thing we all should agree on is that we must fulfill the Great Commission, and we must be salt and light in this world for as long as we remain.

True Education

Possibly the most revolutionary truth of all in the field of education is the most basic truth of all, which is stated in I John 2:27, **"...His anointing teaches you about all things..."** This is the grace and power that has been given to the church with which neither the world, nor any other religion, will ever be able to compete. Think about the implications.

What would happen if every math teacher in Christian schools started teaching math under the anointing? What would happen if every history teacher in our schools started teaching under the anointing of the Holy Spirit? Even math and history would become glorious wonders so filled with the treasure of knowledge and understanding that all who sat under these teachers would develop a passion for math and history which would last the rest of their lives. This knowledge would also be founded on impregnable truth, because the Holy Spirit will lead us to "all truth." This knowledge would also always lead us to a greater revelation of Jesus, because the Holy Spirit was sent to reveal Him.

If math is taught under the anointing, students will end up worshiping God in math class as they see Him in mathematics. As Comenius stated, all true knowledge will lead to the One for whom and through whom all things were made. All true science will lead to the Creator.

Summary

This is quite a long article, but even so, it is a very superficial treatment of this important subject. To adequately address it would require a large book at least, and more likely a number of volumes. Because we **"prophesy in part,"** and **"know in part," (I Corinthians 13:9)** I am presenting only a small part of a huge, panoramic vision for education.

My goal for this message is to at least begin waking up more people to the mandate given, especially to the church, for education. Those who are so awakened have a most important work to do. They will be laying a foundation which can bear fruit for generations to come, even help to lay a foundation for the Great Commission to be fulfilled, and the kingdom to come. Their labor will not be in vain in the Lord.

Psalm 119:160 states, **"The sum of Thy word is truth, and every one of Your righteous ordinances is everlasting."** There are many theologies and eschatologies based on one, or just a few verses of Scripture, which do not take into account those verses which seem to counter their positions. These often-neglected verses may seem like contrasts, but they are not really in conflict with each other, only presenting other parts of the picture.

> As Comenius stated, all true knowledge will lead to the One for whom and through whom all things were made.

For example, there are verses which talk about the way the anti-Christ is going to deceive and subdue, and there are those which talk about the kingdom coming in the time of greatest darkness. There are also some verses such as Isaiah 60:1-5 that show how both are going to happen at the same time.

It seems clear that there are going to be nations that will be almost entirely subdued by evil at the end. There will also at the same time be kingdoms that **"...become the kingdom of our Lord and of His Christ..." (Revelation 11:15 NKJV).** This implies a transition for those kingdoms. If we are Christians it should be our devotion to see that our nation is one which makes this transition, and does not have to be a part of the destruction coming to many. We know that ultimately the whole world will become His kingdom, but there are many texts which indicate a transition.

From these we can conclude that some kingdoms may actually transition to become a part of His kingdom before His kingdom comes to the whole earth. Because the phrase "kingdom" does not necessarily mean a nation, but rather a domain, we can conclude that there are domains of authority which we can take for His kingdom. These could include industries, or even corporations within industries. Of course "kingdom" can also mean a nation, and therefore we should have hope for our nations, and not abandon them to the evil one.

However, even if we are living in a nation which will become completely subdued by evil, or even if we believe that this will happen to the whole world, are we not called to be the salt and light in it for as long as we are here? There are few places where we can be the salt and light for this world more powerful than in education.

For this reason we must start seeing all Christians who are teachers, regardless of where they teach, as missionaries. They can have one of the most powerful platforms for fulfilling the Great Commission. Every Christian who is a teacher, regardless of where they teach, or what they teach, must start seeing this as their ministry—they are to teach "all things" under the anointing.

Though the kingdom of God will not come to the earth until the King returns, we have a mandate to lay a foundation for the kingdom in all that we do here.

Our goal is not just heaven, but to bring heaven to earth. The prayer the Lord Jesus gave us to pray was that His kingdom would come to earth, and His will be done on earth as it is in heaven. The foundation for His rule is now being laid. We are called to prepare the way for His kingdom to come here on earth, and for His will to be done here, just as it is in heaven.

> There are few places where we can be salt and light for this world more powerful than in education.

As Paul the apostle wrote that he was laboring, striving in order to **"present every man complete in Christ,"** (Colossians 1:28) we must take up this same devotion. For this to truly happen there must now be a liberty, a calling rather than a compelling. Even so, our goal is nothing less than seeing every child prepared for their calling in Christ, and to be used to glorify His name all of the days of their life. There is no greater platform for this than through taking over the education systems of the world for the kingdom of God. We know this can only be done by developing schools which are a piece of heaven—so wonderful, so true, so obviously what schools are meant to be, that the world beats a path to our door to get in. ∎

Freedom in Giving

by Dudley Hall

Freedom needs truth like a train needs track. A freight train running across the prairie with no track on which to run is dangerous for its passengers and bystanders. In the same way, people who think they are free but pay no attention to truth are dangerous to themselves and others. Jesus said, **"you shall know the truth, and the truth shall make you free" (John 8:32).** When we are not free, it is because we are either ignorant of truth, or we have failed to embrace the truth we know. Our greatest liberty comes from living according to God's design. God is good and desires to bless us, which He has proven forever on the cross. Rather than trying to live without limitations, we need to access His power by living according to His design.

Everyone I know wants to be financially free, but not everyone agrees on what that freedom looks like. In II Corinthians, Paul wrote chapters 8 and 9 to describe how free people give. He was speaking to these believers about an offering they had agreed to collect and send on to fellow believers in Jerusalem and Judea. Now money is one of those things people avoid discussing in polite company. In church circles we are especially defensive about the subject of giving. But if we find and follow God's design for giving, we can enjoy amazing freedom. We do not have to react to those who try to manipulate us or whose motives we suspect. God wants us to know how to give freely, and these two chapters tell us how.

There is a war for your soul.

To understand the issue of giving freely we must remember that we are in the middle of a battle for our souls over the issue of money. Jesus spoke of material goods in terms of a spiritual power He called **"unrighteous mammon" (Luke 16:11)**. The fallen, spiritual power behind possessions, including money, seeks to destroy the freedom of the possessor. In other words, there is a connection between your stuff and your soul.

> This indicates that the growth of our souls also involves learning how to rightly manage our stuff.

For those of us who have been trained to think that spiritual realities are on an entirely different plane than material things, this is a difficult idea. We can easily understand the spiritual warfare aspects of prayer and fasting, of mission and service, of worship and evangelism, because these are obviously "spiritual." But when it comes to what some call the "real world," we find it harder to understand our budgets, houses, and jobs as in any way relating to our souls.

Jesus spoke in Luke 16 about the progression that occurs in the life of good stewards. He said that those who handle a little well get much and those who know how to use what is unrighteous get true riches. Those who show wisdom in using what belongs to another will get things of their own (see Luke 16:10-13). This indicates that the growth of our souls also involves learning how to rightly manage our stuff. So our discipleship goes beyond

how much we witness or meditate on Scripture, or even how much we do at church, but includes how we use our time, money, and other assets, as well.

Our souls are either cramped or released by how we do these things. Our enemy tries to take good gifts from God and turn them into shackles to bind us. He is behind the many wild ideas out there about wealth and prosperity because he wants to deceive and enslave us. But God wants us to win the battle to be free to enjoy what Paul calls the act of **"grace of giving" (II Corinthians 8:6-7 NIV)**.

Jesus also said, **"For what does it profit a man to gain the whole world, and forfeit his soul?" (Mark 8:36)** If unrighteous mammon has its way, this is exactly what will happen. It's not only a matter of going to hell, but also, of losing out on life before death. There are people who live with dead souls, or who never progress beyond adolescence in their souls. They are handling their possessions in such a way as to gain the world, but they never learn how to embrace genuine life, *by releasing it to others as well*. Their attitude toward their stuff limits the level of their maturity.

Jesus calls the spiritual power behind money and wealth **"unrighteous mammon"** because it pretends to be a god. The spirits behind money try to use it as an idol which puts men into slavery. There are several ways it impersonates God. For one, money outlives us. It also persuades us that its circle of influence is large enough to affect politics and commerce. Wealth has its own sense of mystery that commands respect for those who have it. It lives among the things we worship and it promises some of the same things God's own kingdom offers—things like peace, power, security, and prominence. Such a power must be dealt with as the false god it is, or it will operate unopposed in its deception.

You are created and redeemed to give.

For you know the grace of our Lord Jesus Christ, that though he was rich, yet for your sakes he became poor, so that you through his poverty might become rich (II Corinthians 8:9 NIV).

Paul compares our grace of giving to the grace believers have received from Jesus Christ's giving. He gave up His wealth in order to grant us wealth. We who are born again of that Spirit want to give like Jesus gave. The Corinthian believers whom Paul was writing wanted to give in spite of being far from affluent themselves. The apostle applauds their readiness to give, but he wants them to complete that readiness with implementation. Most of us have experienced wanting to give more than we had to give, and God gives us credit for that desire. He tells us to give according to our means even if we would like to do more (see II Corinthians 8:12).

Before our new birth we lived to get, and even when we gave we thought about how good it made us feel or how our gift might be reciprocated. But **"God so loved...that He gave," (John 3:16)** and believers *who have Him living in them* have His heart to give. When we suppress that heart, we find ourselves in bondage instead of freedom. Creation and redemption is designed within us as a power mechanism which is triggered by our giving. Financial and material offerings are only a part of a way of life that gives constantly and serves creatively. This new way of life compels us to arrange all of life around the priority of giving. Living to give is far better than living to gain, but we must have in order to give.

The great evangelist, John Wesley, was a man of some means who had an experience that changed his strategy for life. A needy woman came to his door one day asking for help, but he had nothing to give her. On his walls hung valuable paintings in rooms furnished with many fine things. He was grieved that he had nothing to give away that would help this woman, and he began to adjust his life to the priority of having money to give. When he died, he had only the money in the pockets of his trousers. He lived and taught a different ethic of wealth: "Earn all you can, live as inexpensively as you can, and give all you can." I think he meant that we should choose a lifestyle that allows us to be content and joyful with less so that others may have more— giving rather than having. There is a lot of pressure to live in luxury just to prove we can, but that is motivated by the power of unrighteous mammon.

> Financial and material offerings are only a part of a way of life that gives constantly and serves creatively.

Giving fulfills spiritual hunger.

As new creatures in Christ, our hearts reflect His extravagant living. We don't care if other people know we have given, only that we have done it. We experience the greater blessedness of being a giver rather than a receiver. This satisfies a deep hunger within us. The danger of mixed motives is largely removed by anonymous giving, and it is also one thing that promotes the growth of our souls. Our motivation for working is transformed by our desire to earn more in order to give more. We are no longer just working for a paycheck but for the privilege of giving.

> When we have no plan for giving, people more easily manipulate us with agendas for our possessions.

A good marker for whether we've entered into the grace of giving is the level of our joy. **"...God loves a cheerful giver" (II Corinthians 9:7).** There are two good ways to move toward joyful and extravagant giving. If there is something in life that seems essential to your happiness, you might as well go ahead and pursue it until you get it. If that trip to Hawaii or that yacht looks like the key to fulfillment, get it out of your system. You'll find it's like cotton candy—it looks much more fulfilling than it is. Do it quickly so that you'll have plenty of time afterward to do what you will value when you have done it. The second way is to make a conscious choice to begin to give extravagantly. Take

care of your family responsibilities and look for opportunities to give.

Spend most of your energy sending most of your wealth where you will spend most of your time.

All Christians claim to believe in an eternal existence above and beyond the one we see around us. We speak of living forever with God in heaven, but the way we handle our belongings gives us a benchmark for knowing how deeply we believe what we say. Jesus says we can lay up treasures in heaven. We can send what we have ahead of us to be kept safely by investing it in the right ways. This is the perspective that transforms financial stewardship. We can convert temporal and corruptible assets into eternal and imperishable things. The problem we have to overcome is that our financial habits are not yet in sync with our hearts. We still use our things as if we had to get all the good out of them before we die.

Advice for converting assets:
1) Give intentionally by faith.

When we have no plan for giving, people more easily manipulate us with agendas for our possessions. For years I couldn't stop at a highway rest stop without someone asking me for money. I almost always walked away not feeling good about what had happened. I had determined to make any mistake in the direction of generosity. However, even when I had given what I felt I could, it seemed like giving by default. I was moved more by appeals than by a sense of purpose. "Intentionality" doesn't preclude some spontaneous giving, but it makes for accountability.

2) Give to those who are needy.

It is very satisfying to give what we have to meet essential and immediate needs for others. If we don't focus on needs, we'll find ourselves interfering with the progress of some people's souls. This usually happens because we don't want to exercise due diligence in our giving. When I am asked for help now, I assume God has sent this person to me because he knew I'd ask some questions. For instance, I'll sometimes ask, "Is this the first time you've been a beggar?" They don't always want to admit that's what they are doing, but I point out that they are not selling any goods or service, so they're begging for help.

Maybe there is something wrong that I can help with beyond money. I'm not trying to be harsh, but I'm using money earmarked for kingdom purposes. Neither do I put any conditions on how to use what I give, but I am not going to help beggars succeed at begging. I consider myself accountable for what I give away, and I think every Christian should experience the blessing of doing this kind of face to face benevolence instead of delegating it all to a committee from the church.

3) Give to those who teach you.

God requires us to reciprocate material blessings with those who bless us with spiritual things (see Galatians 6:6). God has used specific people to bless and edify each of us, and we need to give to these people first. In the Old Testament, each Israelite had a specific Levite who received his tithes, because it was he who taught him the Law. These people need more than money. They need prayer and

encouragement and even friendship. Financial gifts should concentrate on genuine relationships—the two go together. If you are tired of direct mail appeals to give, build a relationship with a ministry by giving various resources in the same direction.

> God has used specific people to bless and edify each of us, and we need to give to these people first.

4) Give to spread the Gospel.

Most readers expect me to deal with the issue of tithing in an article like this. I am really much more interested in presenting a lifestyle than a particular doctrine or practice. Tithing is not a bad place to begin learning the joys of giving, but it is far from the extent of our duty. The New Testament gives us the opportunity to give away everything for the sake of the kingdom, to manage what we have so that we can live as givers. Although I believe that those who teach all kingdom giving should go to a local church have little biblical basis, I believe in giving to my church, and doing it. But our giving has become too centered on pastors and ignoring the support of apostles, prophets, evangelists, and teachers. Most of these gifts are exercised by people who are not on church staffs.

Besides, all of our preaching on tithing has not been very effective. The average evangelical Christian gives less that 2 percent of his income. Kingdom giving includes the church but goes beyond. The model I am presenting will never hurt the churches because believers will be looking to give more not less. Once giving becomes the priority of a Christian's financial strategy, his own church will be the first to benefit.

> # The average evangelical Christian gives less that 2 percent of his income.

5) Give more to fewer.

Scattershot giving dissipates the joy of generosity. If we use a rifle instead of a shotgun, we can focus on a giving agenda consistent with our hearts' passion. Instead of sending a lot of small checks in several different directions, find a ministry or two that is doing kingdom work you believe in most. If we all did this, our ministers would not have to spend so much of their time traveling around to touch base with all their many supporters.

6) Give larger gifts less frequently.

If you are intentional about your giving, you know ahead of time that you intend to give $1200 to a particular ministry. Rather than monthly checks, send it all at once. For one thing, it takes the same time and manpower for an office to process the small check as the large one. But even more important, the giver has more joy in giving a gift that makes an impact. *However, do not let this negate your faithfulness in giving, and if giving more but smaller gifts is better for you, then do that.*

The Bible's perspective on using resources is quite simple. We are to provide for our own families so that someone else does not have to. Beyond that circle of responsibility, we look for ways and places to invest what we have so that it bears the most eternal fruit. Believers will give account before God, not with respect to their sin, which is already covered by what Jesus has done for us, but concerning the stewardship of what God put in our hands. To be prepared for that judgment, we should begin each day asking where we can give money and other assets so that we express God's nature and invest in His purposes.

When we are constantly ready to give, we can expect the Holy Spirit to reveal to us where and how much. There are many good reasons to give:

(1) Others have need of what we have.

(2) We will reap whatever we sow.

(3) Giving transforms our souls. But more important than all,

(4) Giving glorifies God by representing His generous and abundant heart. ∎

Amazing Stories

# of Supernatural Children

by Becky Fischer

It is very encouraging to find more and more people who believe God is going to greatly use, not just the youth, but also children in signs and wonders. These are the days of impending revival and harvest, and the children have a major part to play in it. But it remains to be seen if we are ready for what can happen when we take a pure and sure gospel to a hungry generation of little people. The familiar adage, "anything can happen," certainly applies as you will see in the following stories. These reports are shared to fill you with expectancy of what can happen when children are touched by and yielded to the Holy Spirit.

Stopping Witch Doctors

A friend of my family, Paul Olson, has done much work in the forgotten places of Africa. He has written an excellent book of his experiences entitled, *How to Touch a Leper*. He shared about being invited into a village where he was barred from ministering to adults by the three ruling witch doctors who controlled the villagers. However, they agreed to let him preach to the children.

After several days of teaching on salvation and the baptism in the Holy Spirit, Paul's time there drew to a close. The eighty or so boys and girls had been gloriously saved and filled, and he knew the witch doctors were not going to be happy about it. He knew this could be a life-threatening situation for the youngsters, so on his departure he carefully instructed them, "When the witch doctors come after you, you don't have to be afraid because the power of God lives inside of you. If they try to harm you, simply raise your hand towards them and say, 'I rebuke you in the name of Jesus!'"

INSTANTLY, ALL THREE OF THE WITCH DOCTORS FELL TO THE GROUND PARALYZED AND COULD NOT GET UP UNTIL THEY DECLARED JESUS AS LORD!

Months later Paul heard what happened. The witch doctors began chasing the children with machete-like knives, threatening to kill them. As the multitude of children and teens fled, they suddenly remembered what Paul had told them. They stopped in their tracks, turned to face their aggressors, held out their hands and shouted, "I rebuke you in the name of Jesus!"

Instantly, all three of the witch doctors fell to the ground paralyzed and could not get up until they declared Jesus as Lord! Paul later met one of them who is now a pastor in the same village.

Casting Out Devils

Very close friends of mine, Glorious and Josephine Shoo, run a Christian boarding school in Tanzania for more than one hundred twenty boys and girls. Many

of them come from totally unchurched homes, some are orphaned because of AIDS, and some are Muslim. All are presented with the gospel. Recently, Glorious shared about a boy who was brought to them because he had been kicked out of four other schools for being completely out of control and unmanageable by the teachers. The mother asked if they would give her son a chance. They said they would take the boy, much to the chagrin of the other children.

The students quickly became victims of biting, kicking, pinching, and more. Finally these children, who were born again and Spirit-filled, had had enough. Somehow they came to the conclusion this child had a demon and, without any adult supervision, they pounced on the kid and cast the devil out of him. Suddenly this boy became a model student, and according to my friends, is one of the nicest boys in the school!

Raising the Dead

On my last trip to Africa, I was privileged to meet with a key leader of one of the largest Christian relief organizations, who had spent many years ministering to village children. He shared about two young sisters around eight or nine years old who were home alone one day when their very ill mother died in their presence. The little girls became distraught, weeping and crying in grief. After a couple of hours of this, suddenly the older child sat up, stopped crying, and stopped her sister. "We can't act like this anymore," she said. "Our pastor said God can do anything!" With that they determined to pray their mother would come back to life again.

Instantly the older girl found herself at the gates of heaven, and a large angel stood beside her asking: "Why are you here?"

"Because my mother has died, and I've come to get her and take her home again," the child responded.

The angel reached out and placed a white, glowing ball in the child's hand. With that she was immediately back in her house at her mother's bedside. She placed her hands on her mother, and the woman revived, coming back to life.

Fourth Grade Pentecost

Glorious emailed me a few months ago with a story which left me shouting with excitement because it confirms once again that children can be the instigators of revival. It seems that in a fourth grade, public school class in his hometown of Moshi, situated at the foot of spectacular Mt. Kilimanjaro, a young boy decided to share about the baptism in the Holy Spirit with his classmates. It is a law in Tanzania that public school children are to have one hour of religious instruction per week. The government really does not care which religion it is, so the gospel can be preached openly. But due to a wide range of unfortunate circumstances stemming from the poverty of that nation, teachers don't always show up to classes. Such was the case this day, and so our young friend decided to take matters into his own hands.

The boy began to share everything he knew about the Holy Spirit, and then asked his classmates if any of them wanted to be filled. The whole class responded, and within moments the children were on the floor weeping, shouting, crying out to the Lord, and causing such a commotion that the teachers began running in from other classrooms. One of them, a Catholic nun, decided the children were demon possessed and wanted to find someone to get them delivered. But after about an hour or more, the children began to calm down and told what had happened.

SHE PLACED HER HANDS ON HER MOTHER, AND THE WOMAN REVIVED, COMING BACK TO LIFE.

You're Sick in Your Head!

Another very good friend of mine, Leon Kotze from South Africa, pastors a group of about one hundred fifty children. One boy in his ministry, whom I will call Billy, has been very accurate prophetically since he was about four years old. At that time he actually exposed an adulterous affair going on in their church from what he saw in the spirit and shared with his parents. Pastor Leon took Billy with him to minister in a neighboring church one day and, while they were praying for people at the end of the service, the ten-year-old suddenly began to shout at and shake a woman standing before him. "You're sick in your head! You're sick in your head! You're sick in your head!" He just kept repeating it. Leon came to help and it was discovered the woman suffered from serious depression and had been to many psychiatrists who had not been able to help her. They prayed for her that day, and she was set free.

> WHEN ASKED TO STAND TO THEIR FEET IF THEY WANTED TO RECEIVE JESUS, EVERY SINGLE CHILD STOOD AND PRAYED TOGETHER. THE ENTIRE CLASS GOT SAVED!

Risking Revival in Public School

In November of 2002, Kathy Cavanaugh substituted in a second grade public school in Delaware. After a discussion of what it meant to be thankful, she began to tell the children stories about children in Mozambique, Africa, and the joy and thanksgiving they give to Jesus for just a slice of bread with a smear of jam on it, which they called "a feast." The children were very touched and responsive, and Kathy bravely continued by telling them they needed to give thanks to the Lord for all that He has given to them.

One child said, "You look like you're about to cry." She nodded. Kathy said at that moment, the presence of the Lord began filling the room. From the back, one child said he felt something different. Another boy said he felt a "rushing wind." A third boy looked at her and said, "I can see Jesus right in front of me." Another child added while pointing to a classmate, "I see Him standing in back of you!"

Suddenly the room was electric with the presence of the Lord. Kathy said she was awestruck. Truly the Lord had entered the room and it was a holy thing. She asked Him silently what He wanted her to do, and He said, "Offer them My gift of salvation in Jesus." She did, and the entire class replied with raised hands to receive Jesus, with the exception of one reluctant boy. But when asked to stand to their feet if they wanted to receive Jesus, every single child stood and prayed together. The entire class got saved!

Then the Holy Spirit began to move upon their hearts. One child started to cry because she had lost her PopPop. Kathy felt the Holy Spirit was comforting her. Many of the children began to cry and weep, some from hurts from losses, and others, Kathy sensed by the Spirit, were being deeply healed of inner wounds, while others were carrying burdens of intercession.

Some who weren't crying placed a hand on others who were, offering comfort. One precious girl offered tissues (ministry of helps) the entire hour. Several others ran to the blackboard to express their newly birthed love for Jesus.

Hearts, crosses, love messages to God and Jesus, blessings to the classmates and America filled the blackboard. Kathy shared that her only challenge was trying not to do anything to hinder the moving of the Spirit. She knew God was at work, and she knew better than to touch it or to direct them in anyway, but rather to just let the Lord do what He wanted to do.

Then as the Spirit began to settle the children, someone knocked at the door. "The children are supposed to be in art class," they announced. Kathy lined them up, and laid hands on each one sealing the work of the Holy Spirit, knowing she wouldn't see them again. It should come as no surprise that she lost her job over the incident, but she has no regrets. What an opportunity of a lifetime—to see such a precious move of God on the lives of hungry, little children.

In Conclusion

There are so many more stories that I cannot relate them all. But these are shared to encourage you, whether you are a parent, children's minister, or just care about the move of God in this generation. You, too, can have a front row seat to the supernatural as you train your children, grandchildren, nieces, nephews, and even neighborhood kids about how to hear the voice of God and respond to His leading. What's exciting is these types of stories used to be rare. Today, however, they are everywhere, and it's only going to increase as men and women of God catch the vision, and they begin to see themselves training kids to walk in the supernatural. ■

The best remedy for those who are afraid, lonely, or unhappy is to go outside, somewhere where they can be quiet, alone with the heavens, nature and God. Because only then does one feel that all is as it should be and that God wishes to see people happy, amidst the simple beauty of nature.

—Anne Frank

Mustard Seeds of Wisdom

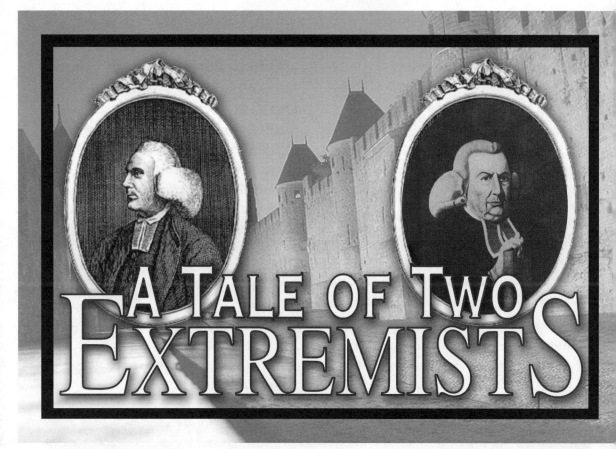

A TALE OF TWO EXTREMISTS

by John Hansen

Instead of ministering the **"gospel of peace,"** (**Ephesians 4:16**), the twenty-six year-old clergyman was being charged with disturbing the peace. After a two-day hearing, the Connecticut General Assembly concluded that the controversial revivalist standing before them was *"under the influence of enthusiastical impressions and impulses, and truly disturbed in the rational faculties of his mind."* They gave him a light sentence: banishment from the colony. The trial ended with the sheriff gently taking the clergyman by the sleeve, *"endeavoring to...remove him."* But in front of everyone the preacher fell to the ground yelling:

"Lord! Thou knowest somebody's got hold of my sleeve, strike them! Lord, strike them..."

Unfortunately, this occasion was only the first of several incidents when this Presbyterian minister, James Davenport (c. 1716-1757), stood trial on charges of religious extremism. His final arrest came the next year, after inciting a riotous book burning. This time, however, it was not the civil authorities, but his fellow Great Awakening revivalists—Jonathan Edwards and Eleazar Wheelock—pressing charges against him. Although Edwards and Wheelock supported the New England revivals, they were not blind to the extremes that accompanied them. In Davenport's case, they had to agree with the critics—he gave the Great Awakening a bad name.

THE OPPOSITE EXTREME

Usually when people think of religious extremism, behaviors such as Davenport's readily come to mind. However, there is another extreme just as dangerous to the purposes of God as Davenport's spiritual "wildfire": Pharisaism. In essence, the Pharisaic extreme occurs whenever we hold an attitude of self-righteousness and inflexibility, which ultimately leads us to resist the Holy Spirit (see Acts 7:51).

When someone with Pharisaical tendencies faces a spiritual work that conflicts with their experience or theology, they usually tend to reject the whole thing, instead of patiently discerning God's heart on the matter. This error of tossing out the proverbial baby with the bath water manifested in one of New England's most respected ministers—and considered the Great Awakening's greatest foe—Charles Chauncy.

To a degree, Chauncy was right about the wildfire extremes of the revivals, and particularly of Davenport. But just as heaven-sent revivals tend to bring out the best and worst in everyone, so the Great Awakening did in Chauncy, surfacing his deep, self-righteous humanism. Thus, this pillar of American Puritanism, in his quest to right the wrongs of the revivals, left himself wide open to a "doctrine of demons" called Universalism—the

parent of Unitarianism.[1] What's more, Chauncy helped pave the way for some of New England's leading churches and institutions, like Harvard University, to embrace this heresy.

> **THE PHARISAIC EXTREME OCCURS WHENEVER WE HOLD AN ATTITUDE OF SELF-RIGHTEOUSNESS AND INFLEXIBILITY, WHICH ULTIMATELY LEADS US TO RESIST THE HOLY SPIRIT**

Chauncy and Davenport represent two contrasting extremes which usually manifest during a major move of God. As history bears out, Satan either uses a frontal assault to try to shut down a move of God (as he tried through Chauncy), or wildfire extremism to drive it off course (as through Davenport). What's more, by looking into the lives of these two extremists we can learn three things:

- How God can restore an extremist for His greater glory,
- What can happen when someone doesn't repent of their extremes, and
- How we can learn to live between the extremes.

---

[1] Unitarianism is a religious association with no official creed, except that God is uni-personal (no Trinity); salvation is granted (not just offered) to all humans; and reason and conscience are the criteria for belief and practice.

THE WILDFIRE EXTREME

How did Davenport wind up going off the deep end? Being a third generation minister, a Yale graduate, and a flaming zealot, he seemed destined for great things. But it was this final ingredient—his untempered zeal—that eventually drove him off track.

> THE REASON FOR THEIR PUBLIC CRITICISMS WAS NOT TO SMEAR ANY CLERGYMAN'S REPUTATION, BUT TO ROOT OUT WORLDLINESS IN THE CHURCHES.

During the two years before his arrests, Davenport converted many people to Christ, and sometimes team-preached with such notables as George Whitefield and Gilbert Tennent. Although his revival message largely paralleled the other revivalists' sermons, something was out of balance with Davenport. As he later admitted, his ministry passion was rooted more in human zeal than in the Holy Spirit's empowerment, making him prone to a "wildfire" religious spirit.

Davenport's downfall began in 1740, when he first witnessed the attention-grabbing effects that Whitefield and Tennent held over their audiences. Davenport noticed, particularly with Tennent, a certain aspect that he considered key to bringing revival. In order to get their point across, the revivalists at times would publicly question the salvation of some established clergymen, calling them "Pharisees."

The reason for their public criticisms was not to smear any clergyman's reputation, but to root out worldliness in the churches. But this tactic backfired on them. Instead of promoting holiness, their denunciations fostered in many an "us-against-them" attitude. It was this divisive theme, along with his promotion of uninhibited emotionalism, that Davenport pushed to the extreme. Patterning after the revivalists, Davenport began branding non-revivalist ministers as carnal and hell-bound. He figured if a minister lacked noticeable fervor, neglected to preach the New Birth, or never experienced a sudden or dramatic conversion, he was unconverted. According to Davenport, that minister's church members were obliged to find another minister.

Many ministers, including Chauncy, admitted that their churches needed reviving. However, Davenport's "revival method" was producing anarchy and enmity in the churches. Inevitably, many ministers became defensive, and some overreacted by judging the entire revival by its extremes. Unfortunately, their critical retaliations opened some of them up to the extreme of Pharisaism, as we will see with Chauncy.

In 1742, Davenport was arrested twice, indicted in part for his late night singing and music marches. Moreover, the church he pastored in New York organized a ministerial council to officially examine *"some irregularities"* in his behavior. An eyewitness of a Davenport meeting reported that his praying and preaching was *"all mere confused medley. He had no text nor Bible visible, no doctrine...I can't relate the inconsistency of it."* In March of the following year, Davenport incited his Connecticut followers to build bonfires for burning their "idols" of worldly clothing, jewelry, and even some Christian classics he deemed spiritually inadequate. Some even reported that Davenport took off his own clothes to throw into the fire! This time everyone, including his fellow revivalists, felt he went too far.

Davenport's unwise antics were only supplying ammunition to the Great Awakening's opponents, who pointed to its disorderliness and divisiveness. Jonathan Edwards went so far as to say that Davenport *"does more towards getting Satan and other opposers an advantage against the work* [the current revival] *than any one person."* Incidentally, when Whitefield and Tennent learned of Davenport's extremes, both men repented of the *"God-provoking and church-rending iniquity"* they inadvertently promoted.

Although Davenport certainly was "zealous for God," his zeal was **not based on knowledge." (Romans 10:2 NIV)** As Solomon wisely said, **"It is not good to have zeal without knowledge, nor to be hasty and miss the way." (Proverbs 19:2 NIV)** Although Davenport was in danger of missing the way, all was not lost for him.

THE PHARISAICAL EXTREME

When the New England revivals began, Charles Chauncy (1705-1787) first saw them as a godsend. Because he pastored the beacon of Puritanism—Boston's First Church—people nicknamed him the "Old Brick." His parents named him after his great-grandfather, who was Harvard's second president. Like Davenport, Chauncy had the makings for greatness. But also like Davenport, he fell into some perilous extremes.

> **DAVENPORT'S UNWISE ANTICS WERE ONLY SUPPLYING AMMUNITION TO THE GREAT AWAKENING'S OPPONENTS, WHO POINTED TO ITS DISORDERLINESS AND DIVISIVENESS.**

In May 1742, Chauncy preached a stirring sermon on everyone's need for an outpouring of the Holy Ghost. But events turned two months later when he received a fateful visit from Davenport. Apparently, Davenport questioned Chauncy about his salvation experience in a manner that offended the "Old Brick." Soon after their meeting, Chauncy carefully crafted a provocative sermon-pamphlet entitled, *"Enthusiasm Described and Cautioned Against."* He prefaced it with a loving appeal to Davenport to change his ways. But he also shrewdly concluded it with a sermon quote from

Davenport's own great-grandfather, who was also Chauncy's predecessor at First Church!

This pamphlet was also the first documented that surfaced Chauncy's humanism. While he accused Davenport and others of being "wildfire" fanatics, Chauncy counterbalanced his argument by stressing, *"the Spirit of God deals with men as reasonable creatures."* Real Christianity, he concluded, was *"a sober, calm, reasonable thing,"* not to be overpowered by our *"passions and affections."* In his attempt to correct the emotionalism in the revival, Chauncy pushed the pendulum in the opposite direction—toward rationalism.

> IN HIS ATTEMPT TO CORRECT THE EMOTIONALISM IN THE REVIVAL, CHAUNCY PUSHED THE PENDULUM IN THE OPPOSITE DIRECTION— TOWARD RATIONALISM.

A month later, Chauncy wrote another pamphlet, claiming the revivals to be the *"effect of enthusiastic heat,"*[2] and that those affected by the revival *"are worse off than before."* As for Davenport, Chauncy labeled him *"the wildest enthusiast* [fanatic] *I ever saw, and acts in the wildest manner."* The following year his fiercest attack came through his pamphlet *"Seasonable Thoughts on Religion in New England,"* which was his rebuttal to the cautious endorsement his fellow Congregationalist pastor Jonathan Edwards gave to the revival.

As the pamphlet war waged between the revivalists and the anti-revivalists (called the "Old Lights"), it was becoming more evident that Chauncy's worldview was growing more rationalistic, believing in *"an enlightened mind."* In short, his religion was more of the head than of the heart. Consequently, by putting excessive faith in "common sense," he set himself up for deception.

DID DAVENPORT CHANGE?

What is often overlooked in the history of the Great Awakening is how God turned the whole wildfire affair around to potentially make the Awakening a purer work. Although Davenport went down in history as an extremist, the rest of his story is rarely told. The moral of his story is not about his extremes, but about God's power to restore people.

After the bonfire incident and a season of suffering with a debilitating sickness, Davenport humbled himself and heeded correction given by his brother-in-law Eleazer Wheelock. In July 1744, Davenport took a further step toward restoration by publishing in

---

[2] "Enthusiasm" is an old derogatory term for "an overly confident or delusory belief that one is inspired by God." Its origin is from the Greek word "entheos", meaning "having God within." (Taken from *The American Heritage Dictionary of the English Language*, Houghton Mifflin Company, 2000.)

the *Boston Gazette* an apology for his extremes. He started his recantation by affirming how God graced him and others with *"special assistance and success"* to lead many to Christ. But he also admitted that after *"mature consideration,"* he recognized two factors which drove him off the deep end: a misguided zeal and a false spirit.

> I am now fully convinced...that several appendages [extremes] to this glorious work are no essential parts thereof, but of a different and contrary nature... which appendages [extremes] I have been...instrumental of promoting, by a misguided zeal; being further much influenced by the false spirit...

He then addressed his particular extremes, with his rash criticisms of other clergy topping the list:

> [T]he method I used...with respect to...many ministers...in openly exposing such as I feared or thought unconverted,...offending against the laws of justice and charity [love]...by my advising and urging to such separations from those ministers, whom I treated as above, as I believe may justly be called rash....

Next, he humbly admitted that his unchecked enthusiasm pushed him beyond the bounds of Scripture:

> I confess I have been much led astray by the following impulses... whether they came with or without a text of Scripture, and my neglecting also duly to observe the analogy of Scripture...[T]his was a great means of corrupting my experiences, and carrying me off from the word of God, and a great handle which the false spirit has made use of with respect to a number, and especially me.

HE (DAVENPORT) RECOGNIZED TWO FACTORS WHICH DROVE HIM OFF THE DEEP END: A MISGUIDED ZEAL AND A FALSE SPIRIT.

He also dealt with his irregular singing episodes. On the surface, it seems petty for him to include this issue in his public apology. But Davenport was not repenting of his singing, but of his abusing the **"law of liberty" (James 2:12)** in Christ. He knew his singing was culturally offensive, so he should not have let his freedom become an offense for others (see I Corinthians 8:9).

Finally, he repented for being the *"ringleader in that horrid action"* of books and clothes burning. *"I was... under the powerful influence of the false spirit, almost one whole day together... although I thought...that 'twas the Spirit of God in an high degree."* Apparently, the Lord showed him his ministry passion was fueled more by *"impatience, pride* and arrogance." His recantation concluded with a sober exhortation for people to "*learn to distinguish the appendage* [extreme] *from the substance or essence...*"

AFTER PUBLISHING HIS CONFESSION, DAVENPORT VISITED THE PASTORS HE PERSONALLY OFFENDED.

A BROTHER RESTORED

After publishing his confession, Davenport visited the pastors he personally offended. In fact, a few days before publishing his apology, Edwards told Wheelock that Davenport "*is much fuller of the Spirit of God than he was in years past when he seemed to have such a constant series of high elevations and raptures.*" He was on the road to recovery.

For the next ten years, Davenport's life, when compared with his Great Awakening days, seemed virtually uneventful. Although he pastored a few churches and conducted some evangelistic campaigns in Virginia, God had more in store for him. In 1754, a decade after his recantation, Davenport was installed permanently as pastor in New Jersey. Soon after, his fellow Presbyterian ministers honored him with the post of Moderator for their annual Synod meeting of churches. What probably thrilled the heart of the "Singing Evangelist" the most were the revival stirrings occurring in his church and the region.

Although he died three years later at the young age of forty, God was still not finished with restoring Davenport's name. Almost twenty years later, his son John became an ordained minister, and for a time filled the pulpit of the very church that once called a ministerial council to examine his father's former "irregularities"! Truly, Davenport's life exemplifies God's mercy and restoration power.

DID CHAUNCY CHANGE?

Ten years after the Davenport episode, Chauncy, out of reaction to the "terrors of the Lord" emphases of the revivalists, developed a theology that was unorthodox. Writing to a relative in 1754, he confided how he "*made the Scriptures my sole study for about two years; and I think I have attained to a clearer understanding of them than I ever had before...The commonly received opinions* [on Paul's Epistles] *are quite remote from the truth.*" Turns out, what he really attained was a Universalistic interpretation of the Scriptures. Universalism is a belief that everyone will eventually go to heaven, and it strongly emphasizes the perfectibility of man. Subsequently, it rejects the cardinal doctrines of the new birth and eternal damnation.

That same year, Chauncy drafted "*The Salvation of All Men Illustrated and Vindicated as a Scripture Doctrine,*" the first of his Universalistic works. Here he claimed that all men eventually go to heaven, because a loving God could never eternally damn anyone. Therefore, why should anyone bother evangelizing? According to *the Dictionary of Unitarian and Universalist Biography*, Chauncy surmised that every *"soul would be disciplined or educated in a period following death… [Then] the soul would be ready for eternal holiness and happiness."* This theology is nothing but a repackaging of Satan's lie from the Garden, **"You surely shall not die!" (Genesis 3:4),** and unfortunately, the "Old Brick" bought into it.

For almost thirty years Chauncy kept his draft under lock and key, deeming it too radical *"to admit of publication in this country."* When he finally published it in 1782, America was ripe for the picking, riding high on the Enlightenment's rationalism and optimism. The next year he followed up with *"The Mystery Hid from Ages and Generations Made Manifest by the Gospel-Revelation."* He wrote, *"I was at first brought into this train of thought by being willing, in opposition to previous sentiments and strong biases, to follow the light wherever it should lead me."* Shortly before his death, he released two more Universalistic works.

Eventually, Chauncy's First Church and two hundred fifty other Colonial churches—like First Parish Church, which the Mayflower Pilgrims founded—all succumbed to the spirit of the Enlightened Age. Today many of these same churches are still displayed in the trophy room of Unitarian-Universalism. Sadly, many today admire the "Old Brick" as one who led New England out of its supposed Dark Age of Christian ignorance and into the "light" of humanistic religion.

If only Chauncy had continued with his initial pro-revival stance, and learned to wisely distinguish the move of God from the extremes of people, who knows how many more people could have been touched by the revivals? Instead, this one-time defender of the faith opened the door for what later became the greatest threat to New England's *Second* Great Awakening—Unitarianism.

> THIS ONE-TIME DEFENDER OF THE FAITH OPENED THE DOOR FOR WHAT LATER BECAME THE GREATEST THREAT TO NEW ENGLAND'S *SECOND* GREAT AWAKENING—UNITARIANISM.

LIVING BETWEEN THE EXTREMES

Davenport believed emotions and experience had their place in the Christian walk—and he was right. Chauncy believed reason had its place—and he was also right. But what is the balance between them? Years after the Awakening revivals subsided, a much wiser Gilbert Tennent saw the proper place for emotions and reason. *"Light* [reason] *and heart* [emotions] *are inseparable companions to religion, without the latter the former is cold formality; and without the former the latter is wild enthusiasm…"*

As Christ said, true devotion to Him will always include our emotions *and* our intelligence, our hearts *and* our minds (see Matthew 22:37).

So, how can we prevent ourselves from taking anything spiritual to an extreme? For starters, we must realize that, from time to time, we all tend to see things in extremes. We all have misjudged people and events based on our limited knowledge and wounded emotions. In addition to studying the Bible, the key safeguards to our living between extremes are our walking in Christ's humility and love. Consequently, when we cultivate His humility and love in our hearts, His wisdom will inevitably come (see Proverbs 11:2; 8:1). Then, with these three virtues in hand—humility, love, and godly wisdom—we can safely stay within biblical parameters.

Furthermore, in our quest to not squelch any work of the Lord, we need to follow Paul's rule of carefully examining everything, learning to extract the good from the bad (see I Thessalonians 5:19-21). The sooner we walk in Paul's standard, and in the wisdom, love, and humility of Christ, the more likely God will use us to protect future revivals from the consequences of extremism. ■

BIBLIOGRAPHY

Chauncy, Charles, *Enthusiasm Described and Cautioned Against*, Boston: J. Draper, 1742.

Davenport, James, *The Reverend Mr. James Davenport's Confession And Retractions*, Boston: S. Kneeland and T. Green, 1744.

Webster, Rev. Richard, *History of the Presbyterian Church in America*, Philadelphia: Joseph M. Wilson, 1857.

For questions or comments regarding this article, please contact John Hansen at MPIServices@aol.com

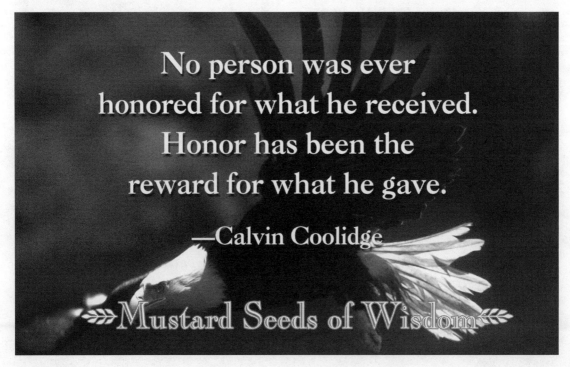

No person was ever
honored for what he received.
Honor has been the
reward for what he gave.

—Calvin Coolidge

Mustard Seeds of Wisdom

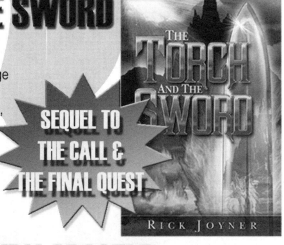
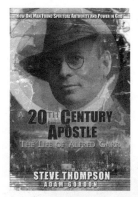

MST
MorningStar Strategic Team

MST is a special fellowship of those who have joined with us in heart and action for our purpose in these times.

To become a member of MST requires that you make a monthly contribution of $15 or more, or an annual contribution of $150 or more.

For your convenience we will send you a self-addressed envelope each month. You may also authorize monthly credit/debit card deductions.

Please call 1-800-542-0278 for more information on how you can join. You may also join on our website at: www.morningstarministries.org

CSCL

MorningStar Lodge

New Church Site

Youth Camp Site

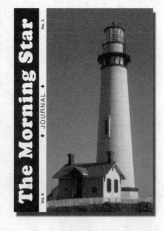